He that travelleth into a city before he hath some entrance into the language, goeth to school, and not to travel.

—Francis Bacon

Black Jargon
in White America

by

DAVID CLAERBAUT

WILLIAM B. EERDMANS PUBLISHING COMPANY
Grand Rapids, Michigan

To Erwin and Wilma, Alyce and Rochelle

Acknowledgments

My sincere thanks to Steven Woods, Cornelius DuBose, Keith McDonald, Coy Davis, and Bill Owens, all of whom selflessly contributed to the compiling of the dictionary. They deserve much credit.

A special note of gratitude is extended to Marlin Van Elderen and William Whitney. Mr. Van Elderen willingly involved himself in reading an earlier version of the manuscript and offered some helpful remarks on it. It is hard to imagine how it would have been completed without his dedicated efforts. Mr. Whitney contributed in the indispensable area of motivation and encouragement. His continual willingness to aid in any way possible was of great help.

There are many others who helped too. Among them are Mrs. Betty Lavengood, my conscientious typist; Mrs. Elizabeth Teicher, who gave me the benefit of her knowledge in many areas; and Dr. W. R. Dixon, who was of much help when the research for this work was done.

Oh yes, I should also like to thank the students and teachers who provided me with many of the experiences I relate from memory in this book.

Foreword

Black Jargon in White America is a simply written account of a form of communication readily understood by most black Americans, but largely ignored until recently by most white Americans. This book was written by a white American who was willing to look deeply at his own frame of reference and acknowledge that his lack of understanding of black jargon was in reality a lack of understanding of black Americans who use that jargon. The author's genuine interest in people and his consequent frustrations with his initial teaching experiences in a predominately black school "led him to the mountain" and enabled him to develop some significant insights into a problem he shares with most white Americans.

This book is not intended for black Americans, though they will be interested in the ideas set forth and could undoubtedly provide some "advanced schooling" in a number of the ideas and jargon discussed. Rather, *Black Jargon in White America* addresses itself to those white Americans who spend some part of their lives working with black Americans, but who rarely take the time to find out who the black American really is. White teachers and other professionals who work in urban or inner-city schools should find this book particularly helpful.

The writer's accounts of his experiences, though not meant to be prescriptive, do tell how teachers fail to get their students tuned in to learning. The dictionary of jargon contains a range of terms used in various sections of the country. The difficulty in any compilation of slang or jargon terms is that there is constant change in words and their meanings. Nevertheless, a review of the jargon and the more commonly accepted meanings might provide a framework for understanding more deeply the black Americans who know, use, and continue to create new terms and expressions from their "soul" experiences.

Most of the ideas in *Black Jargon in White America* are not at all new. Even the dictionary of jargon is not unique. But what is refreshing is that here one reads the insights of a white American who took the time to listen, to learn, and to understand.

—Dr. Gregory A. Morris

Pittsburgh, Pennsylvania

Contents

Preface

Jim: What's happenin', mellow?

Bill: You got it, brother.

Jim: Hey, man, last night after Ken split from his crib, some dude ripped off his box and all his bad jams.

Bill: Anyone see the cat?

Jim: Yeah, the gray broad downstairs said he had a Deuce and a Quarter. Hope they bust him, man.

Bill: Right on, brother.

Jim: If Ken meets him he says he'll be thumpin' not rappin'. He ain't frontin', man.

Bill: I can dig it, Jim ain't jivetime. *wak* ⟨It's 1992⟩!

Jim: We'll see you at the gig, mellow.

Bill: Solid, brother.

If you understood the preceding dialogue, this book is not for you. If you didn't, you may learn something about one of the major features of a completely different way of life. For this dialogue is in the language or jargon of black America.

The first question that often comes to mind is why a language so different from that of white America? After all, black people are exposed to the language of white America in virtually every area of their lives. Don't they watch the same television programs? Don't they travel through the same school systems? Don't they live in the

11

same cities? They do. But for the most part they do so together—as residents of the all-black areas of cities, as members of the Black Student Associations in colleges, as roommates and eating partners on many big-league teams, as black pupils in this nation's inner-city schools, or as those "colored guys" (or worse) who constitute an ever growing segment of the labor force in America's factories and offices.

In any case, they are largely isolated either by choice or design from the wider society. They exist together as victims of the formerly overt, but now more subtle, oppression of white America. They exist alone, drawn together by the unmistakable badge of blackness.

Black people have lived in this country for well over 350 years. Only during the past 100 years have they been officially free. This means that they have lived mainly as slaves for at least 70 per cent of their existence in this country. In other words, another 150 years must pass before black Americans will have spent even half of their existence in America as legally free citizens. It is little wonder, then, that black people are hardly throwing their arms around members of the white majority at the first sign of a lessening of prejudice and hostility. Black people have learned to be distrustful, an adaptive mechanism designed for survival. A series of social changes—many of them superficial—is not likely to reinstate trust in a people who have been conditioned to distrust for over three and a half centuries.

White America has only recently begun to adopt a policy of treating black people fairly. But a beginning is all it is. This fact was impressed upon me in a rather amusing but saddening way on my honeymoon. Because my marriage is interracial—I am white and my wife is black—and because it is difficult to find lodging in the Chicago area on weekends, I decided to call in advance for motel reservations. I did, and reserved a simple room for two. So with a feeling of security, my wife and I made our way to Chicago after the wedding. When we got to the motel and our room we were surprised by a bouquet of flowers and a bottle of champagne standing on the desk. We liked the room, and the next day decided to stay an additional night. That evening I entered the office, and as I looked at the newspaper rack, the woman behind the desk asked who I was.

"Claerbaut," I answered.

"Oh," she exclaimed, "so you're the newlywed!"

"Yes, I am," I replied shyly.

"Well how did you like the flowers and champagne arrangement?" she bubbled.

"They were very nice, we really were pleasantly surprised," I returned.

"Oh, I'm so glad," she gushed, "because they were my idea!"

"They were? Well, thank you very much," I answered.

She then continued, "You know, we all had a big laugh about the whole thing, too."

"How's that?" I asked.

"Well you know you called your reservation in," she explained.

"Yes," I said.

"Well, after setting the whole thing up we said, 'You know, wouldn't it be something if we'd gone through all that work and then they'd turn out to be colored people?' "

That the battle against racism has hardly been won is evident in countless areas of life. One can easily see this by observing the painfully slow pace at which our national and city governments move to eliminate injustices; the prevailing attitudes that cause the value of a house to continue to be determined on the basis of how near the closest black family lives rather than on its structural worth; and the continually derisive references to "the niggers" or those "blankety-blank colored people"

13

that are still present in many conversations of exclusively white groups. Even that growing number of people who wish to become aware and who sincerely seek change tend to retain many of their unconscious racist attitudes and instincts while seeking awareness. This is only logical when one considers the violent, hate-soaked, white-over-black, segregationist history of this country. We are all products of it and therefore conditioned by it. It must be realized that segregation breeds ignorance, ignorance breeds racism, and racism breeds hate. Nevertheless, there remain people of goodwill who genuinely want to contribute to better race relations. I have met housewives, businessmen, laborers, ministers, students, and teachers who truly want to be liberated from their racist shackles. And it is for such people—however unsure, however unintentionally patronistic—that this book is written.

The central purpose of this book is to demonstrate, first through a series of autobiographical sketches and later in more depth, that effective verbal communication is fundamental to any success in race relations. But this communication must be truly two-way. For this to occur, white people must come to learn and appreciate the jargon of black America—a unique and fascinating jargon through which many black people communicate.

Chapter I

I first became interested in black culture when I did my student teaching in a virtually all-black urban school. When I began, I felt optimistically eager and prepared for the novel experience. My mind was full of high-sounding thoughts and opinions. After all, I liked black people; some of my best friends were black. I disliked racial prejudice; I believed in equal opportunity for every citizen. I was all for helping black students learn. In addition to these attitudes, I had already had a good deal of experience with black people. My credentials included having worked in a black church; having coached a multiracial basketball team of juvenile delinquents as well as a predominantly black group of Little League football players; and even living in an integrated neighborhood.

I entered Eastern Junior High School* with a real desire to help the students. I felt I could really teach these young people something. It didn't make any difference to me whether they were fast or slow learners. I was confident that, given the space of one school term, I could mold them into the kind of people I felt they should be. With a little enthusiasm and dedication much could be accomplished. All they actually needed was a bit more education and cultural refinement and they would be

*I have used pseudonyms throughout this book.

able to fit quite well into the white society. They really lived much as I did. There were some differences, but these were easily accounted for by ignorance and the lack of a favorable background. I knew they would be a bit hostile at first, but that was natural and expected. Students are always hostile toward a teacher at the beginning. I could endure that. The real issue was whether I could handle the material in such a way as to make it meaningful for the students. If I could do that, the hostility would quickly disappear and we would get along well. That was my challenge as I marched into Eastern Junior High School to begin teaching. I was assigned to teach several sections of ninth-grade civics. As I entered Room 703 my eyes met those of John Brock, who would counsel and supervise me in my efforts whenever necessary.

"What's happenin', Dave?" Brock said, greeting me with a grin. John was a handsome black man who was very popular with the students. I had observed his entertaining teaching methods several times and hoped to emulate them. He made his room very attractive to black students. The back wall was alive with a galaxy of blow-ups and posters featuring everyone from Godfrey Cambridge to Robert Kennedy. I was happy to see a room decorated like that for a change. I had seen too many drab academic settings in the inner city, where children existed as strangers amid depressingly blank walls, or even worse, bulletin boards designed to honor and glorify only white, middle-class heroes.

"I can't wait to get started, John," I said eagerly to Brock. As we talked, students intermittently strolled into the room, flashing suspicious glances at me as they sat down. When the final bell rang, Brock left the room. It was up to me now. I stood up to greet the students, confident that they would be impressed by a young, contemporary, outgoing, white teacher like me.

"Hi, my name is Mr. Claerbaut," I began. I sensed a

16

deadness so I hurried on. "Mr. Brock wants me to teach in here for awhile," I said, trying to identify quickly with a popular figure. The students' response to this introduction fell far short of my expectations. They either groaned or said nothing. Theresa Brock's eyes bore in on me as I spoke, her expression indicating offense at my very presence in the room. Marie Bonner viewed me with a "so-what" air. Mitchell Morgan didn't even bother to look up.

Aware of this total lack of communication, I could feel a gentle form of panic setting in. I was determined not to let it show, however. It would be defeat of the worst kind to tip my nervousness to them the first day. No, I had to keep my poise and carry on. I did and somehow endured the first day.

The next days were to prove no better. From the outset the students talked, laughed satirically at amusing goings on in class, and generally exhibited very little respect for me. It was very unsettling, and I began to realize that playing the nice guy would be suicidal. It became increasingly obvious that I was charming to no one. Dale Carnegie could hang his hat. I had to be tough. After all, if these people were going to be so unfair as not to accept me at face value from the start, how was I to know that they wouldn't move from passivity to action and attempt to take over the classroom? I resolved to rule the class with an iron hand; I would tolerate no nonsense. After all, I was there to teach and they were there to learn.

Leo Karls, slouched in his seat, with his gigantic boots in the aisle, was one of the early targets of my new offensive. His attention always seemed to be fixed on whatever he could see through the window overlooking Harrison Street. Disgusted at his apparent indifference, I decided to go after him. "Look, Leo, you have to pay attention if you're going to get anything done in here," I reprimanded. Time was to reveal that Leo never did care

17

whether he accomplished anything or not. In fact, he produced nothing during my entire teaching tenure, and at this particular moment Leo remained lifelessly slumped in his chair, quite oblivious to what I had said.

"Sit up, Leo, you heard me!" I shouted desperately. Slowly and painfully, he drew his feet out of the aisle and straightened himself in his seat.

I also got on Don Applewine, who sat directly behind Leo. Don was small and wiry. He regarded me with a passive hostility. His lethargic appearance camouflaged a quick wit, which he demonstrated at my expense when I caught him talking with a neighbor.

"Quiet, Don. We can't get anything accomplished in here when you're talking!" I commanded.

A normally listless Don whipped around and blurted, "O.K. man!" in punch-line fashion, eliciting gales of laughter from his appreciative audience.

With the class in an uproar, I cried, "Please, people, let's cut down the noise!" The group finally did come to order, but the fact that they hardly regarded me as having a great deal of charisma was embarrassingly obvious.

As the days passed, I could tell I was getting through to very few of the students. They rarely responded to me in a positive fashion. Instead, they would carry on discussions among themselves when the class was in session. Often, in fact, the kids were so unruly that I was forced to add to the chaos while pleading for order. I might begin with an "All right, people, let's calm down," which developed into a "Settle down, please!" and eventually degenerated into a shrieking "Quiet!"

But while the students were hardly held spellbound by my teaching methods, I did seem to be reaching some of them. It appeared that Mary Stark was one of them. Mary had early distinguished herself as a bright, cooperative, and very popular student. It was very comforting to feel that an intelligent girl like Mary not only recognized me as an affable, fair-minded person, but also held me in high esteem.

One day, after a particularly frustrating experience of trying to quiet the class, Mary raised her hand. "Go ahead, Mary," I said eagerly, anticipating some much desired support.

"Mr. Claerbaut, we don't learn anything in here. All you do is holler and shout at everybody. It makes me sick!"

"Yeah!" the group sang out in unison. Once again, my confidence had been misplaced.

All right. So high-handed authoritarian methods weren't very successful, but my attempts at a controlled discussion proved no panacea either. During the course of our civics study, the question of riots and their effects arose. I felt this would be an excellent topic to discuss. Newspapers, nationwide, had shown the devastation of riot-torn areas. I firmly believed that for people to pursue their rights was basically honorable; but there were legitimate and peaceful channels they could use to achieve their goals. Looting, burning, and other violent acts were certainly not among them. I was convinced that no one could really condone such destructive behavior, especially after witnessing its damaging effects.

Dee Dee Wilson, a boisterous and very opinionated young lady, didn't feel this way. She loved to indulge in tell-it-like-it-is oratory and waved her hand frantically. I called on her expecting the worst. She didn't disappoint me, as she began in vibrant form. "Man, those riots really were somethin'. They sho' scared a lot of them honkies around here. They be runnin' outta the streets, into their houses, and lockin' their doors." The class loved her style, and Dee Dee, wagging her head vehemently with every critical point, pressed on. "Yeah, and that ain't all, neither. Everybody got in 'em 'cept them Uncle Toms that be runnin' around with white women all the time."

"But, Dee Dee," I reasoned, "are riots the best way for people to get their rights?"

"Well I ain't sayin' it's the best way, but black people been tryin' to get treated decent for hundreds of years; and there ain't been nuthin' that's worked better and quicker than the riots, that's for shore!" Her peers joyously endorsed her statement while I stood mute. I had bungled an excellent opportunity for a meaningful discussion and then been harpooned by a ninth grader's stinging rhetoric.

John Brock had instructed me to fuse some English with the civics material. He wanted the students to get an opportunity to apply specific English skills. But, he continued, standard English should be taught as a foreign language to black students, as they have a nonstandard language of their own. Surely, I thought, the situation could not be as extreme as that. Nevertheless, since English was my specialty I gladly consented to teach it. I brought the point up before the class. "The main reason Mr. Brock wanted me to teach in here was because I have a background in English." Sensing the ever present hostility and resistance, I decided to win their approval by launching a mild diatribe against the always unpopular English Department. "Because Mr. Brock feels some students are not really getting enough worthwhile knowledge from their English classes, he wants me to work some English into our civics unit."

The response was less than enthusiastic. "This ain't no English class."

"Yeah!" screamed another rebel. "We don't want no English in here."

"Well," I said, passing the buck, "since that's what Mr. Brock wants me to do, I'll just have to do it."

"Aw shoot!" Dee Dee Wilson grumbled as the rest of the class moaned. Once again, I had proven no politician. The students were not duped by my attempts to pacify them. I had underestimated a perceptiveness common to the entire culture, the ability to read through insincerity with deadly accuracy. It is a skill developed by necessity through the years, a valuable defense against the dishonesty and exploitation which black people have endured throughout their entire experience in America. I began to realize that I'd have to be more genuine if I was going to have any chance of being effective.

Theresa Brock was another story. She viewed me with such bitterness and resentment that she would literally snort at most of my suggestions. Once she raised her hand and queried, "Mr. Claerbaut, how long are you going to be teaching in here?"

"Probably for several months, Theresa," I replied, trying not to flinch.

"Ugh!" she sneered.

She was brilliant and learned with minute perfection every column inch of the material I presented. But her classroom mastery seemed to spring from one basic motive—to prove that there was nothing I could give her that she could not handle. She exhibited her hatred for me at every opportunity, and it was for this reason that I tried to avoid asking her questions in class. Nevertheless, I couldn't ignore her altogether. "Theresa, what term do we use to describe literature used to influence people?"

Theresa coldly stared me in the eye, drew her lips back tightly against her teeth, and slowly said, "Prop - a - gan - da," spitting out each syllable with vengeance.

"Very good, Theresa," I replied, hoping that somehow my insincere compliments would sweeten her disposition. Needless to say, they didn't.

I never did understand what was eating away at her until Brock filled me in. "Theresa is a relative of mine. Her family and mine are very close. She really resents the idea of anyone's teaching in my place. Theresa's stubborn. She'll never give in. Don't let her bug you, though. If it gets bad, just ignore her."

It was bad already. Ignoring her was impossible. She *was* bugging me. Occasionally, I'd attempt to salve my ego and hide my frustration by announcing, "I don't care whether any student in this room likes me or not. As long as you learn the material, I'm satisfied." I was not a very fast learner. Though I had repeatedly been stung by their perceptiveness, I still failed to operate with this skill in mind.

Even my attempts to relate to their social interests resulted in chaos. I noticed fashion-conscious Mitchell Morgan's nylon socks one morning. I knew black people had certain distinctive dress-styles and that black nylon socks were popular among the guys. Brock had called them thick and thins. In an anxious attempt to be relevant, I remarked, "Got the thick 'n thins on today, huh Mitchell?"

"G-got the woolens on today, h-huh man?" Mitchell stuttered back with a grin. The class howled with glee. Even slow-learning Mitchell Morgan had put Mr. Claerbaut down.

In spite of my many difficulties, there was a brief period when we were progressing through the civics material quite steadily. This granted me a large measure of satisfaction. I knew that in the last analysis much of my superiors' evaluation of me would be based on the students' academic progress.

However, even this success was short lived, as I soon fell on hard times once more. The subject matter of the civics unit was the presidential campaign of 1968. It didn't excite the students very much. I was trying to move through it as quickly and smoothly as possible, for I sensed their disinterest. Some of them felt wholly disenfranchised by the American system in general, while other, less disenchanted students simply saw no great political savior among the candidates in that particular election. The students' disdain, however, was further compounded by the way in which I covered the material. Brock had made up an entire unit outline and I unwisely presented it through lectures and the use of the blackboard. We scarcely began Richard Nixon and a student raised his hand: "Hey, Mr. Claerbaut, are we going to do much more of this jive? I'm getting tired of this stuff."

"I realize it may be a bit difficult at times," I replied, trying to sound understanding, "but we do have quite a few more candidates to go yet and . . . "

"I hate this stuff!" Theresa shot out.

"I'm not doing no more of this. This is no fun," hollered Dee Dee.

"Yes, Dee Dee," I quietly returned, "but school can't always be fun . . . "

"We *never* have any fun in here anyway," grumbled another dissident. That obviously marked the end of that particular method of teaching that subject. I discussed the mutinous situation with Brock and he felt that although the lectures should be scrapped, the material still had to be covered. It seemed that the only way to accomplish this was to get the students more actively involved. The next move, then, turned out to be an attempt to buy them off by letting them learn the issues through role playing. Individual students played the various candidates, giving speeches while the others hooted and hollered their sentiments at them as part of a political audience. The students were initially very resistant to the role-playing activity, but realizing that the alternative would probably be the lecture form, they grudgingly cooperated. With loud candidates and noisy political audiences we all survived the unit together—itself a major accomplishment.

The crowning insult, however, was taking place behind my back. One by one, the kids were going to Brock, and saying "Hey, how come you don't teach us no more?

That dude we got now don't know what's happening. You gotta get rid of that dude and come back."

By mid-term the students were really getting to me. I was having no effect on them, but they were having a devastating effect on me. I dreaded walking into the room each morning, and I was beginning to get desperate. I was disintegrating in front of them, but what was so much worse, they knew it; I could sense their zealous efforts to accelerate the disintegration process. Swallowing my pride, I turned to Brock for help. "What should I do, John? I tell them to do something and they refuse. They won't even learn the material. The kids are driving me up the wall, man. I never thought it would come to this, but I'm losing control!"

I could see it was puzzling John. He suggested a number of alternatives during our discussion, but one thing he said stood out: "I don't know what you're doing, but you must be doing something wrong. You must be doing something that's turning them off."

But what could it be, I wondered? I had tried from the outset to be friendly, often going out of my way to greet students in parts of the building other than the classroom. I had certainly been reasonable in my dealings with them. Despite all the disruptive activities that had occurred during my tenure in Room 703, I had not sent a single student to the office because of his misbehavior. In addition, I had allowed tremendous freedom of expression in the classroom.

How could this be happening to me? I could get along with white junior high students. These ninth graders were kids too, after all. Black maybe, poor maybe, but nevertheless kids. They weren't really any different. Perhaps I had made a few mistakes, but certainly they were forgivable. All in all, I felt I could characterize myself as a young man with lots of energy and full of good intentions.

Good intentions, however, were not enough. There *was*

definitely something wrong. And the kids had pinned it down when they told Brock I didn't know what's happening. I didn't. I had been teaching a group of young people about whom I knew nothing. These students ate different food, lived in different housing, enjoyed different activities than I did; they even talked a different language. Much of my problem was that I hadn't been concerned enough with these differences to find out what they were or how they could be bridged. Instead, I had joined the legions of inner-city teachers who pay lip service to dedication, but whose work day ends when the final bell rings. A group who, almost to a man, use as their favorite defense the time-worn credo, "My job is simply to present the material. It's the kids' job to listen and learn it."

I hadn't mastered the most basic skill of teaching. Lucian Davis has written: "The teacher's first problem is to communicate."[1] My experience had proved him correct. Teaching required, above all, communication, and I hadn't communicated. I didn't know how to communicate. I had been operating like many politicians, who believe that merely by spending an afternoon or evening in the inner city they can get the pulse of a people whose mood and outlook have been formed by over three hundred years of oppression. It was time to get involved in the nitty-gritties of these students' lives—to learn what life is like in their environment, on their side of town. It was time to make some phone calls, visit some homes, and do some reading and talking, but most of all a great deal of listening.

[1] Lucian Davis, "Can You Dig It?" *California Teachers Association Journal,* LXV, No. 3 (1969), 19.

Chapter II

In view of the difficulties I was having, I was happy for the occasional opportunities I had to visit Brock at his home. I recall one incident in particular. The evening began graciously enough but the climate slowly changed until I found him burning my ear off. "We're sick of being called 'they!' Our mothers gave each of us a name. We're always being told about ourselves. White folks keep categorizing us and defining our terms!

"The news is the same way. If a white dude holds up a store the announcer describes him as 'a man 5-10, medium build.' If a black man holds the same place up, he says 'a *Negro* 5-10, medium build.'

"Black people know white people but white people don't know black people. That's why all the myths. Black people are violent. Black people are dirty. Black people are stupid. Black people are lazy. Yeah, and best of all, black people have tails. Most of those people don't even know any black people.

"You think much of what has happened to us is our fault. In the final analysis, all our problems can be traced back to the white man. Go ahead, name something that can't be traced back to the white man—that actually is our fault!"

I couldn't think of anything. In fact his barrage had me so stunned I would have considered it a major accomplishment if I could clearly state my own name at that moment. Before I had any chance to reply, he tore in again.

"Nothing, man! All this comes from slavery. White people brought us over here. They made us work in their cotton fields. They broke up our families, beat down our people, and then years later, after still not accepting us, they wonder why all the trouble. Why don't they lay off." I was beginning to feel very uncomfortable about teaching in the inner city.

Then he really dug in. "Look at the white teachers. They come down, work a few years and then take off. They don't get involved with the kids at all outside of the classroom. THEY DON'T EVEN KNOW THE KIDS' LANGUAGE! The kids and I could talk for a whole class period and a white teacher wouldn't understand a bit of it."

Such expressions as "dude," "what's happening," "jive," and "honkies" were certainly not part of my background. But an entire class session conducted in black jargon? Unimaginable! How could any inner-city group, made up of basically English-speaking people, possibly have a vocabulary which varied so greatly from the standard English spoken by the middle class? Questions such as this raced through my mind. Nevertheless, as my experience in the inner city grew, his claim made more and more sense to me. It was not long before many interesting and unique examples from the black lexicon began turning up in my experience. It became evident that this difference in jargon is critical, for it is the lens through which one can view a completely different way of life—an American subculture.

Tragically, these variances are not perceived in this way by white America. When I began in the inner city, I felt I came in free of prejudice of any kind. But as experience forced me to take a closer look at myself, I worked my way through layer after layer of my liberal veneer. At first I enjoyed the process, for I uncovered many shining examples of laudable behavior, from my involvement in a black church to my volunteer efforts with a largely black athletic team. I was not, therefore, prepared for the shocking discovery at the core of my outlook. Despite all the trappings of fairness and decency, despite all my good works, I still clung to that most universal and prejudicial of all American myths—that white is superior. And that belief, existing as it did amid a wealth of good intentions, made me an impediment to the progress of black people everywhere. Once I had adopted this belief, I had struck myself blind to "what's happening." Instead of accepting and respecting the black students' cultural differences, I had, like millions of other white people, been making subconscious judgments upon these differences. . . .

Such a judgmental attitude, however unintentional, is invariably damaging to any attempt at successfully dealing with others. William Green, using the language of black students as an example, pointed out this very weakness when he strikingly asserted that the teacher whose students come from a different culture will gain nothing until he learns to couple acceptance and respect with understanding when dealing with them. The use of all three of these components is vital:

> Rather than feel condescending toward the language of culturally different children, the teacher must respect and understand their language if he is to win their confidence and overcome their hostility to standard speech.[1]

I had been unable to appreciate the beauty of these differences in language and culture; unable to see that they reflect the creativity of an oppressed people. These differences indicate the ability of an enslaved people, ripped out of their native land and excluded from the mainstream of American culture, to develop a fascinating

[1] William D. Green, "Language and the Culturally Different," *English Journal,* LIV, No. 8 (1965), 729.

life style truly their own—a subculture in which language is, of course, a basic ingredient.] Let us take a brief look at a few facets of this subculture.

Black people are no less individual than whites. Therefore, many of these cultural differences, though common to the experience of vast numbers of black Americans, are not applicable to all. But even if they do not characterize the life of certain segments of our black population, these segments are still well aware of the existence of these characteristics and are influenced by them.

The black family throughout history has been unique enough in its structure and function to have necessitated entire academic courses designed to study it. One of its primary distinguishing features is its expanded structure. To many black children, the term "family" does not mean simply "mom, dad, sis', and brother," but may well refer to grandparents, uncles, aunts, and cousins as well.

This extended aspect proves valuable to many black children. Often the black child's immediate family is subject to poverty, death, illness, or other calamities—any or all of which tend to break or at least severely strain the immediate family bond. The fact that the divorce rate is high is easily explained by the almost impossible pressures under which many black families exist. A father who is a victim of unemployment and who has little stake in the future and little more than token respect from the economic and socially powerful wider society often is virtually driven from the home by these conditions. Much of the debate concerning the welfare system has for years centered around its tendency to encourage a family to break up so that it can receive aid. Poverty and family life do not mix well. What is really remarkable is that so many marriages do last, and that families remain together despite these devastating conditions. In any event, the family's first objective, then, is not to lay aside money for country club dues, a suburban home, or even a college education—but to survive. And survival may mean placing a child in a relative's home or, conversely, rearing a cousin whose parents died or whose house burned down. Whatever the case, the geographical presence and the genuine concern of the extended family is a positive and valuable asset.

To survive, the low-income, victimized, and exploited black family must be mobile. Residential transience is pretty much the rule rather than the exception. For example, in one year more than 90 per cent of Eastern's approximately 1,100 students had moved to a new residence at least once. Poor living conditions, high rent, and unstable income make this pattern necessary.

In this rugged environment, black society tends to be more physically oriented than white society. This is hardly surprising. Spawned in slavery and its torturous physical labor, blacks still have to be physically tough and resilient to endure in the midst of poverty and social deprivation. Fights and scuffles among black children are frequent and are looked upon as normal. This is a culture of the street, not of the meadow or the plush lawn.

Black people often have to do without the most basic physical necessities. I recall the example of Nora Logan. Nora often slept in school during the mornings. She was intelligent and able to read well, and yet she could scarcely stay awake and function in my class. That Nora was poor was evident from her dress. What clothes she had were old, and they fit so poorly that they could not have been bought originally for her. Concerned about her inattentiveness, I decided to call her mother. I found her polite and honest. Nora slept because she lacked energy. And she lacked energy because she was hungry. She ate no breakfast at home, then walked to school ill-clothed in all types of weather to face an entire morning with an empty stomach. Her problems did not stop there. She often ate no lunch because she could not afford a meal-ticket. Tragic? Yes. Unusual? No. I contacted the principal and got her a mealticket for the remainder of the year.

Roy Farrell was a sixth grader. I talked to him one day in the teachers' lounge. He fidgeted around nervously as we discussed various things together. The conversation eventually turned to food. Roy said he got hungry a lot, but he didn't let it bother him too much. He said he was used to it because a lot of times he didn't get enough to eat.

Within such an atmosphere there exists an acute awareness of death. Whether due to illness, poor diet, violence, or some other cause, it is common to the everyday experience of many inner-city residents. Death is treated as a serious, often tragic, but nevertheless very common occurrence. This ever present reality exists in the minds of even the younger inner-city children. This was impressed on me one day when I was working with a group of sixth graders. Mike Billings was late for a class after lunch. When I asked him why, he explained. "See, there was this man just up the street and he was laying in the yard, dead in the snow. See, some kids robbed somebody at Grocery Holiday and when they ran away they knocked the man over in the snow. He was under the snow when they found him today. I saw him. He was stiff and his skin was yellow and he was dressed up except his shoes and socks were off. He was real old. He lived a few houses away from me."

This report led to a discussion of death. Ann Logan, a serious A- student, raised her hand and told of another stark experience. "Last summer I was walking down Davidson and I was by a store and I saw this man laying up next to the door. I said, 'Look, Mommy, there's a man and he's dead.' She looked and he was dead, and she said we should call the police. We did and they took him and he's buried now." She went on. "He looked like he'd been drinking. He smelled like it. He was laying under a coat right up by the door."

Perhaps the most jolting look I received into the reality of death for blacks came in an experience I had coaching a group of sixth-grade football players several years ago. One day, Butch Lester, a tough, quiet, and coachable kid, was not at practice. I asked where he was and one of the players explained. "He won't be here, his father was stabbed to death last night in a fight." What surprised me as much as the news was the matter-of-fact way in which it was related. Such incidents did not seem to shock them. In a day or two Butch was back. "I wasn't here," he said, "because I was at my father's funeral." That was that. With no further ado, he returned to the business of playing football.

On a brighter note, food is a part of every culture, and black culture is no exception. One would be hard pressed to find a black family that is not aware of and does not eat soul food. Soul food reflects the history of black America just as do many of the other aspects of the subculture. It is basically inexpensive food consisting of many types of meat, vegetables, and other items that have for years been rejected by more affluent Americans as undesirable. Yet black people have made the most of what they have been left with, and as a result many soul food dishes have become famous and in demand in various parts of the white society. About three times a year, a nearby black church would prepare soul food dinners and sell them to our staff during lunch hour. Those were big days for the church and Eastern Junior High.

Much has also been said and written about the black church. My experience attending and working at Lantern Chapel in Milwaukee has been a very uplifting experience. What is most striking is the emotional component of black Christianity. It does not take long to witness the depth of feeling and emotion that is so much a part of the religious experience of the black believer. It is refreshing and challenging to hear loud singing, vocal amens, and other expressions of genuine involvement on the part of the people as they worship the God on whom they depend for spiritual strength in an unfeeling environment. This dedication and commitment contrasts strikingly with the bland indifference that characterizes so much of American "Christianity" today.

A great deal of attention has also been focused on the exploitive "rich, black preacher in the poor black church." But Lantern Chapel is no different from many other small congregations, and there the pastor worked faithfully for twelve years, while holding an outside job in order to feed his family. When one thinks of the many men like him, the stereotype of exploitation loses its impact.

Moving in another vein, one notices that uniquely black styles and approaches are permeating ever more areas of life. Black influence and reality are being felt. And it is healthy. It is psychologically beneficial for an individual to express his identity clearly and with effect. It is no different for a group. For the groups we belong to aid us in our search for identity. This expression is especially healthy for a people which has been a victim of three and a half centuries of individual and group suppression, second-class citizenship, lesser opportunities, and lack of respect and dignity. "If you're black, get back" is no longer acceptable, as the bushy hair styles, bright-colored dashikis, and other visible cultural expressions of black pride indicate.

Finally, let us turn to one of the major areas of cultural expression in which black people have been involved for a long time—the world of music. The black musician is a key figure in black American history, and soul music is one of the black man's greatest artistic expressions. He communicates the black way of life through its sound and lyrics. Hardly anything is more popular with black youths than soul music. They respond to it by soul dancing—a highly developed art form. My real introduction to it illustrates how much cultural difference there can be between people of different backgrounds.

Early in my teaching tenure at Eastern I decided to attend one of their after-school dances, hoping it would give me more rapport with my students. I walked into the cafeteria and there they were, turned on as I'd never seen them, coming alive to the sounds of their hero, James Brown. I was lined up against the wall trying desperately to look at ease until cute, bright, and vibrant Marie Bonner came up to me. "Come on, Mr. Claerbaut, let's dance. I'll dance with you."

"No, this is your dance, Marie," I replied, praying she wouldn't press the issue.

"Please, Mr. Claerbaut, come on, let's dance."

She reached for my hand and led me out onto the floor. A mass of heads turned. I had never even seen soul dancing before, much less attempted it. I knew how to dance by white, rock standards, but soul dancing was a different world. I was inwardly praying that the record player would break so I would be spared this agony. It didn't and I wasn't. Marie was understanding. She started dancing slowly and conservatively. I tried a few moves but it was no use. I felt and must have looked like an arthritic giraffe. Things didn't improve either, for the song was really moving now and Marie was moving with it. There was no place to go, and I could feel one pair of eyes after another turn toward me. I was locked into a situation in which I was making a fool of myself with every beat of the song and every ill-timed step I took to keep abreast of it. Finally I called out desperately to Marie, "Hang it, I'll dance the way I know how—like white people dance."

I did, and it must have made for a ludicrous scene, Marie and I dancing not only different dances but out of totally different cultures. Nevertheless, it was a hit for the students. I had been coveting anonymity on the dance floor, but anonymity was a lost cause now. A crowd began to gather, until out of the approximately 200 people on the floor, only two were still dancing— Marie and I. The rest had formed a huge circle, clapping their hands, yelling out, and enjoying it immensely. "Hit it, Mr. Claerbaut—go." "Is that the way *you* dance?" "Do you know that man?" "Out of sight!" It was a mixture of praise, taunts, and incredulity. When the song ended, I nodded a quick thanks to Marie and retreated hastily to the nearest corner.

Many black people, as well as many social scientists of both races, feel that such differences constitute more than merely two different views of life or two different American experiences: they constitute two separate worlds. It is not surprising, then, that there is a profound difference in language between the two cultures.

Chapter III

Black vocabulary is one of the keys to exploring the entire world of black culture. For after all is said and done, the vital factor necessary to learn another culture is the ability to communicate with its members. And language—especially vocabulary—is the medium of communication. For whether you are a resident of an integrated area and want to get acquainted with your black neighbor, a sports fan in a stadium sitting next to a black person, a participant at a biracial party, a school teacher in a mixed or predominantly black school, a worker with black co-workers, or just an individual who wants to increase his knowledge and awareness of the people around him, it will be most advantageous, if not necessary, to get to know their grass-roots jargon.

But the mere fact that there is a uniquely black jargon or "jive" does not mean that *all* black people employ it. In fact, though black people in all age groups converse in it, it is especially used among young black Americans. Nor may we assume that because a black person uses this vocabulary he is therefore unable to use standard English effectively. Such assumptions are patently false and racist. Many blacks are fluent in both languages or dialects.

It is true, however, that blacks often have to learn

standard English almost as a foreign language.[1] In the light of this, it seems incredibly unfair to expect black people to speak our language everywhere—as employers, employees, bus passengers, students, and acquaintances— particularly while we choose to remain ignorant, and even worse, disinterested in their jargon—a jargon which is easy and fascinating to learn. The point here is not that standard English should not be taught to and learned by all Americans. But why should standard English necessarily be the only truly acceptable language, the only recognized language, and in many people's minds, the only real language? It is precisely such thinking that makes those who do not naturally speak standard English antagonistic toward learning it. Black people, after all, communicate very well with their own vocabulary. Still, to many it is unacceptable, not merely as a formal language, but as an informal jargon as well. In our schools we appreciate the various dialects and vocabularies of Spanish, German, French, Dutch, Swedish, and even Latin, but we often do not regard the black dialect— pronunciation, grammar and especially vocabulary—as legitimate.

That there is a linguistic difference between black and white people was noticed as early as 1913 by an examiner of the renowned Stanford-Binet intelligence test. For this reason the examiner modified the vocabulary used in the test to minimize the difference.

> The author, who apparently obtained all the testing results herself, reports that in the administration of the tests, a few changes from the Goddard revision were made, such as substituting "doctor" and "preacher" for the words "physician" and "clergyman."[2]

[1] William A. Stewart, "On the Use of Negro Dialect in the Teaching of Reading," *Teaching Black Children to Read,* ed. by Joan C. Baratz and Roger W. Schuy (Washington, D.C.: Center for Applied Linguistics, 1969), p. 168.

[2] Wallace A. Kennedy, Vernon Van De Riet, and James C. White, Jr., *The*

Actually the issue of whether a uniquely black speech pattern exists has been under debate for decades. William Labov attempted to come to grips with that issue when he wrote:

> The most careful statement of the situation as it actually exists might read as follows: *Many features of pronunciation, grammar, and lexicon are closely associated with Negro speakers—so closely as to identify the great majority of Negro people in the Northern cities by their speech alone.*[3]

Educators discovered long ago that black children and other poor children often "do not speak the 'language of the school'."[4] As a result, an additional myth arose to go along with the myths of black laziness, stupidity, immorality, and the rest. It was the myth that black children suffer from an extreme language or vocabulary deficit. Frank Riessman, though not accepting this belief as valid, refers to it when he states:

> A great deal has been said about the language, or verbal, deficit supposedly characteristic of disadvantaged children. It appears that agreement has been reached that these children are inarticulate and nonverbal.[5]

Though many intelligent people, including educators, remain unenlightened, the notion that inner-city children are nonverbal has been thoroughly discredited. Martin Deutsch, in studying this matter, concluded that the

Standardization of the 1960 Revision of the Stanford-Binet Intelligence Scale on Negro Elementary School Children in the Southeastern United States (Tallahassee: The Florida State University, 1961), p. 35.

[3] William Labov, "Some Sources of Reading Problems," *Teaching Black Children to Read,* p. 33.

[4] Eunice Shaed Newton, "Planning for the Language Development of Disadvantaged Children and Youth," *The Journal of Negro Education,* XXXIV, No. 2 (1965), 172.

[5] Frank Riessman, "The Culturally Deprived Child: A New View," *The Education Digest,* XXIX, No. 3 (1963), 14.

lower-class child is quite expressive but is simply not adept at syntactical construction:

> . . . In analysis of expressive and receptive language data on samples of middle- and lower-class children at the first- and fifth-grade levels, there are indications that the lower-class child has more expressive language ability than is generally recognized or than emerges in the classroom. The main difference between the social classes seems to lie in the level of syntactical organization. If, as is indicated in this research, with proper stimulation a surprisingly high level of expressive language functioning is available to the same children who show syntactical deficits, then we might conclude that the language variables we are dealing with here are by-products of social experience rather than indices of basic ability or intellectual level.[6]

Roger Schuy reinforces Deutsch's conclusion in his analysis of the claims made by several teachers that inner-city students are limited in vocabulary. He asserts that investigators in this area simply mishandled interviews with students and therefore drew erroneous conclusions:

> This reflects a widely held but erroneous concept, in which the disadvantaged child is sometimes called non-verbal. Nothing in the current research on Washington, D.C., or Detroit Negroes supports this idea. The notion that children in disadvantaged homes are the products of language deprivation seems to mean only that the investigators proved to be such a cultural barrier to the interviewee that informants were too frightened and awed to talk freely, or that the investigators simply asked the wrong questions.[7]

Schuy's statement graphically reflects what often happens when a person from one culture tries to converse with a person from another without taking into account

---

[6] Martin Deutsch et al., *The Disadvantaged Child* (New York: Basic Books, Inc., 1967), p. 71.

[7] Roger W. Schuy, "A Linguistic Background for Reading Materials," *Teaching Black Children to Read,* p. 120.

the cultural differences. What arises is clumsy communication or no communication at all. This scene is re-enacted daily in factories, schools, churches, and public events wherever black and white people are together.

Sidney Trubowitz, who has written an entire book on teaching in a ghetto school, approached the verbal ability of the children from a positive standpoint, pointing to the expressive use of language as one of the ghetto student's greatest strengths:

> Many children in the ghetto display a knack for expressive language. A child who describes a hole in a sock as a "potato in the shoe" and a child who sees a cloud as "the color of ham fat" both reveal an ability to use expressive language. Children who can insult each other with a neat turn of phrase are not totally without language ability. This use of highly figurative language, understood only by the initiated, may be the children's way of showing their power over society and authority.[8]

And Frank Riessman, who has perhaps done more than anyone else in the study of the culturally alienated, has this to say:

> . . . Is not this too simple a generalization? Aren't these children quite verbal in out-of-school situations? For example, that the educationally deprived child can be quite articulate in conversation with his peers is well illustrated by the whole language developed by urban Negro groups. . . .[9]

It is important not to miss the point that some of the jargon tends to have a regional flavor. Eunice Newton alludes to this fact when she writes that "during [the student's] formative years, his verbal environment . . . [is] permeated with . . . [a] profuse use of regionalisms, slang,

[8] Sidney Trubowitz, *A Handbook for Teaching in the Ghetto School* (Chicago: Quadrangle Books, 1968), p. 89.

[9] Frank Riessman, "The Overlooked Positives of Disadvantaged Groups," *The Journal of Negro Education,* XXXIV, No. 2 (1965), 162.

and cant."[10] The term *fimpted,* for example, may be popular and common among many black people in Detroit, but virtually unheard of in Chicago. This fact would likely account for the scarcity of expanded, multi-regional dictionaries dealing specifically with the vocabulary of America's inner cities.

In any case, the jargon, indeed, exists. But most white inner-city school teachers are inadequately acquainted with it. I gained a bit of firsthand knowledge on this subject through some research. While doing graduate work I decided to determine how well Eastern's white teachers and white student teachers know the jargon of the black community in which they teach. I arranged over 150 examples of the vocabulary into a multiple-choice test and administered it to various groups in the school. The results were rather striking. The average score of the twelve black teachers tested, all of them in at least their second year of teaching inner-city students, was 85 per cent. Three of them got over 95 per cent of the items correct. The poorest score was 73 per cent. The twelve white teachers tested, each also at least a two-year veteran, averaged only 69 per cent—poorer than the lowest black teacher's score. The best performance was 83 per cent, with the worst being 38 per cent, a score which dragged down the average significantly. The eight white student teachers managed a 64 per cent average. Their range was not as wide as that of the white teachers—the best performance being 80 per cent, with the poorest attaining 56 per cent.

I count as one of the more fortunate experiences of my inner-city teaching the help I received learning something about black jargon. My black students and colleagues were very willing to help me once I admitted my ignorance, and I found the jargon not only fascinating but immensely valuable. In fact, beginning to learn black

10 Newton, *op. cit.,* p. 171.

jargon marked the turning point in my efforts to communicate with and be accepted by the students. A delightful cycle began to emerge. The more jargon I learned, the greater were the dividends in enjoyment and communication. The greater the dividends, the more I sought to augment my knowledge.

An experience with Jerry McDowell illustrates this. He was sitting next to me during one of the basketball games. Now Mack had not exactly distinguished himself as a potential Rhodes scholar in my class, but he was a delightful fellow. He was ineligible as a player during the first semester and informed me that I'd have to wait till second semester to see him in action. He was engrossed in the pre-game warmups when one of the Eastern players leaped up and stuffed the ball through the hoop. Mack became flooded with excitement. I turned to him and asked, "What do black people call a dunk, Mack?" His eyes swelled with delight. "A cram, Mr. Claerbaut!" he exclaimed. I felt a sense of full acceptance at that instant, and the feeling was exhilarating.

Although the use of black jargon can bring positive results, it is wise to do so with discretion. There have been many times when I have been able to use it advantageously—to clarify a point in a largely black classroom, to express an idea informally whenever the atmosphere seemed to be right for it. But to use it glibly, as though one were black or some sort of a "blue-eyed soul brother," often serves only to alienate black listeners as well as make an obvious fool of oneself.

This potential for alienation must not be overlooked. For although certain terms found in black jargon have been common to the informal vocabulary of many American groups, a vast number of once uniquely black terms have in recent years been pirated by white society, especially by the white youth culture. Although imitation is often considered the highest form of compliment, and although a certain amount of cultural interchange is natural, such indiscriminate theft is deeply resented by many blacks. I am uncomfortable when I hear young whites glibly using originally black terms like *rap, right on, hip,* and *uptight,* as though they have been imported directly from white northern Europe along with the rest of the culture. This thievery is evident even in the media, as the use of black jargon by white entertainers is a common practice on radio and television. Moreover, there has been an upsurge of white pop music groups who attempt to imitate black singing groups by singing soul music in black fashion.

Piracy of the jargon and style does not end here, however. Whites have even stolen certain black customs. For example, whites have not only taken on the habit of *slapping five* but are, as one black teacher pointed out, even engaging in the black-power handshake with fellow whites.

It seems that much of this represents a naive attempt to identify with black people and form some sort of meaningful bond. It requires little insight, however, to understand that such practices hardly bring about this idealistic objective. Stealing a man's culture is hardly a way of befriending him. Respecting it does. And herein lies a critical distinction. It is valuable—in fact it is essential—to any white who wants to relate to black people to learn much of the jargon of the black culture. However, learning it should be done in an effort to understand and better communicate with black people; it is offensive merely to skim off the most appealing terms and then indiscriminately assimilate them into white slang.

Proper use of the jargon by whites can help to bring about a positive situation, for it indicates a genuine attempt to communicate on the black man's terms. This is a refreshing change. Whites don't usually operate this way. The majority rules, even in social situations. Hence, white terms prevail. However, when one can demonstrate a knowledge of and respect for another man's informal language, then meaningful communication becomes possible.

By communication, I am referring to genuine, eye-level communication. We can easily communicate over the store counter, at the office, or at a business meeting. Such interactions hardly bring about the sincere, enriching dialogue on which solid personal relationships are built. Instead, talk in those situations is often contrived on both sides, the circumstances usually demanding only minimal cooperation and socially acceptable behavior from all parties so that each can accomplish his own ends. In such an atmosphere, black people are hardly encouraged to communicate, as there is often little regard for anything but white cultural values and behavior patterns.

Obviously, there is no one way for a white person to effectively use his knowledge of black jargon. To suggest a formula would be silly and presumptuous, for to do so would be to stereotype black people, in effect to categorize what remain individual reactions to an issue. Some black people want no part of any nonstandard English form and much prefer to communicate in standard English only; others, especially members of the younger black generation, relish dialogues heavily loaded with black jargon. Obviously, then, it is best to feel out the situation rather than set forth a tightly structured set of do's and don't's. Often it is wise to begin by exhibiting a spirit of acceptance, respect, and encouragement in regard to communication in general, through the means of good listening rather than talking. Once this mood has been set, one can resolve to use the jargon whenever he feels or perceives that it is warranted and valuable in the communication effort.

It is also well to realize that learning black vocabulary can spare one from the embarrassment of unintentionally offending black people by ignorant uses of the jargon. Blithely to assume that love and concern can adequately compensate for inappropriate language is hardly rational.

Clare Herald and Lillian Barnes, using examples from the environment of the school, allude to the tragic results that ignorant, improper or careless use of the jargon may have:

> Most particularly, when teachers don't "pay a mind" to the language they use with Negro students, they can become offensive. Certain everyday teacher language used in mediating everyday student behavior, carries special meaning for the minority culture. Just as the majority culture would be offended to hear a male student publicly call another male a "fairy" so also would a Negro male be offended if addressed as "punk," to him a synonym for fairy.[11]

Putting aside the issue of the possible bad repercussions which may emanate from improper use of the jargon, it is wise to seriously consider the remarkable potential that learning the vocabulary has for improved racial relations. It would be naiveté at its peak to assume that racial disharmony would disappear in its entirety if only there could be better verbal rapport. Nevertheless, better verbal rapport is a vital step. For when we really ponder it, we have to agree with what Langston Hughes once said: "My motto as I live and learn, is dig, and be dug in return."[12]

[11] Clare Herald and Lillian Barnes, "Hey, Boy!" *Elementary English*, XLVI, No. 3 (1969), 263.

[12] Kenneth S. Goodman, "Dialect Barriers to Reading Comprehension," *Teaching Black Children to Read,* p. 28.

Chapter IV

As with so many other aspects of black American culture, black jargon has its origin in slavery. William Grier and Price Cobbs, in their book *Black Rage,* refer to the sophisticated methods employed by white slaveowners as they attempted to prevent any communication among the slaves. The imported slaves came from various tribes. Each tribe had its own way of life differing from that of every other tribe. The slaveowners realized that to allow imported slaves coming from the same tribe to remain together constituted a real danger. The slaves could band together under the oppression of their dehumanizing conditions and plan and conceivably execute a successful rebellion. The slaveowners thus took measures to eliminate this potential threat, separating and scattering slaves from the same tribe in order to remove any basis for verbal communication. In addition the slaves were not taught to read or write. Communication, as far as the owners were concerned, could not serve a very useful purpose anyway, for manual labor did not require a high degree of literacy. One can easily see, then, that a very thorough effort was expended to destroy any possibility of a slave's continuing to identify with his cultural heritage. Each slave was truly a man without a country and practically a man without a past.

The language the slaves were exposed to was English,

but only by way of the ear. Their masters usually taught them only as much English as they needed to communicate in the fields. Yet, little by little the slaves did pick up English words by hearing their owners talk. But when the slaves tried to pronounce some of the words they often came out twisted and garbled. These mispronunciations formed the basis of a whole new communication system. The slaves cleverly began to turn this language to suit their purposes and, though they didn't realize it at the time, were on their way to developing a dialect of their own. This emerging dialect provided the slaves with a valuable defense against the oppression of the alien environment. This twisting of the white man's words enabled them to communicate their feelings to one another without being understood by the oppressive slaveowners, who regarded these unusual word modifications merely as the inept attempts of a bungling group of slaves to learn the well-developed English language. Along with the garbled pronunciations, many of the words were invested with more than one meaning to further insure that the communication would be exclusive to the slaves. As their vocabulary enlarged over time, the slaves were actually laying the verbal groundwork for an emerging subculture.

It is from these roots of alienation, then, that black jargon arose. It has not stopped there. The jargon has grown, and in the twentieth century it continues to develop. The modern era, however, has seen the advent of several new forces in the development of a black vocabulary. One of these is the black musician. The blues and soul musician has, through the years, loaded his art with the message of the black American experience—a message with which masses of black Americans can identify. And he has made his message truly black, truly soul, by relating much of it not in standard English and conventional terms, but in a vocabulary best understood and best appreciated by black people. And as the black musician keeps creating and developing his art, the black jargon through which he transmits much of it continues to develop and grow.

Another important force helping this vocabulary grow is black humor. There are always a host of jokes which are exclusively black in their origin and nature and often remain in the subculture. These jokes are usually told in the latest jargon of the black community.

We have observed that the language of the slaves provided a common ground for them. In doing this, it also contributed to the development of a distinct identity. A common language is a rallying point, a distinguishing feature of a group. It is an element peculiar to the group which uses it, and as such, provides the group with a certain degree of uniqueness and exclusiveness. Again, it must be remembered that a very destructive and systematic attempt was made to strip the slaves of any positive identity or uniqueness. But the slaves refused to be destroyed as a people, overcoming this almost unendurable experience by pulling together and developing a language system, a life style, and therefore an identity truly their own.

It is not surprising that a peculiar jargon continues to serve that identity function for many black Americans today. Many ethnic groups seek to preserve their ethnic identity by speaking in terms native to their ethnic group when in the company of fellow members of their own background. They derive great satisfaction from the use of their native vocabulary. So it has been and is with black people—stripped of their African culture, tribally separated, dehumanized through slavery and ongoing discrimination, they have also ingeniously developed and used a dialect of their own—complete with pronunciation, grammar, and especially vocabulary—to stamp their unique identity indelibly into the mind of America.

Beside providing a sense of unity and identity, black dialect functions as a critical element highlighting the separation of black culture from white. When we remember that it was white oppression which made it necessary for black people to develop their own modes of verbal communication, it is very easy to understand that much of the emerging jargon is often a way of expressing hostility for whites.

It is often difficult to trace the terms of black jargon back to their origins or roots. There are several reasons for this. First, black jargon is constantly changing, constantly evolving. But more important, much of the jargon is transmitted verbally rather than through literature.

Nevertheless, a look at the jargon instantly reveals the remarkable ingenuity of the people. Upon close examination one notices that many of the words and phrases have, by direct or indirect means, been cleverly adapted from words and phrases used in the wider society. Some are rather apparent as to their origin or reference while others are fascinatingly complex. Here are some of them:

Brim; lid; sky piece: These refer to a hat or other headwear. It's not hard to see the logic of these definitions.

Vines; threads; rags; fabric; weave: All of these denote clothes of some kind. The point of *vines* is that vines often serve as a covering—on a building, for example.

Kicks; floorburners; boots; stompers: All of these obviously refer to shoes or other footwear. *Skis* is used humorously to denote a very large pair of shoes.

Bad—means good, desirable, or stylish, illustrating the tendency of black jargon to contradict the attitudes of the wider society.

Uptight; tight cheeks; tight jaws: Each of these refers to anger.

Get your nose; nose open: These allude to the male condition of being in love or strongly infatuated with a woman to a degree which makes him unable to exercise his own will in the relationship. He has a ring in his nose.

Sheen—a short form of the word *machine,* which in turn refers to a car.

Joy juice—means alcoholic beverages.

Pluck—means wine and refers to the plucking of grapes.

Deuce and a Quarter: This very widely used phrase refers to a Buick Electra 225.

Stalks—means legs.

Building—a person's house or place of residence. The word reflects the impersonality with which black Americans often regard their living quarters, since home-ownership is difficult if not impossible for many of them.

Hat up—means to leave, alluding obviously to putting on one's hat and coat.

Vacation—means to be in jail. It is a sad but humorous commentary on the poverty of many black people that the only vacation many of them get is in jail.

Liberate—to steal something, to remove it from the possession of the business establishment.

Rap—means to talk or communicate. One of its possible origins is the word *rapport. Silent rap* is a communication or rapport gained without the use of words.

Ig—to ignore or avoid someone.

Creeping—being disloyal to one's spouse or loved one. It refers to the secretive nature of such disloyalty.

Splash—taking a bath.

Woofing—a threat not to be taken seriously; refers to the proverbial dog whose bark is worse than his bite.

Bogart—a bully or physically aggressive and combative person; comes from the name of the actor Humphrey Bogart, who often was cast in such roles.

Doberman—means a traitor or doublecrosser. The word is taken from the Doberman pinscher, a dog notorious for suddenly turning on someone without provocation.

Oreo—comes from the cookie of the same name; refers to a black person who acts black but thinks white.

Spotlight: This denotes a light-skinned black female. It

is derived from the spotlight-like appearance that she casts when paired with a dark-skinned male.

L-7: This is among the most ingenious of the terms. It means to be unable to relate to others; to be out of place; to be "square." If one puts the figure of a capital *L* together with a *7,* the two form a square.

Tom; Uncle Tom: These well-known terms denote a black man who is a traitor to his race by identifying himself with the white race in his attitudes or actions. Its origin is the title character in Harriet Beecher Stowe's famous novel, *Uncle Tom's Cabin.*

Soul brother; brother; soul sister; sister; blood: Each of these refers to a fellow black person, regardless of age or geography. The word *soul* indicates a special depth of feeling, and each term points to the unique cohesion, unity of experience, and identity shared by black Americans.

The vocabulary is complex and flexible. The size of the vocabulary itself is one clear indication of this. In addition, it is adaptable enough to accommodate the use of various combinations of terms. Take, for example, the expression *a laid crib.* The word *laid* means stylish, while *crib* means house. Hence, the phrase refers to a nice house. Similarly, the expression *bad rags* refers to attractive or nice clothes.

A *hammer* is a female while a *nail* is a male. Therefore the phrase *hammer and nail* means a boy and a girl—a couple. Similarly, a *mellow nail* is a stylish man while a *fine hammer* indicates an attractive female.

The adjective *gray* is used in many phrases. It refers to a Caucasian, a white person. Hence, a number of combinations arise, all referring to white people—*gray dude, gray broad,* etc.

Like standard English, black jargon forms many of its words simply by adding the suffix "ing." The word *brick* becomes *bricking,* throwing bricks. *Game* becomes *gaming,* attempting to impress, to deceive, to manipulate. The word *z's,* which refers to sleep, becomes *z'sing,* sleeping. Also like standard English, the jargon uses the prefix "un." It is not uncommon to hear the words *unhip, uncool,* or *untogether* to suggest that a person or experience was undesirable or "square."

Black jargon reflects black culture in many ways. Poverty is as native to the black American experience as almost anything could be. However, if one is without money, it does not mean he is unaware of money. On the contrary, often this deprived state places an additional value on it. Poor people often have great interest in the materials that could alleviate this condition. This is very evident when one observes the many words that denote money in black jargon. *Scratch, jack, dough, pounds, change, bread, lettuce, cabbage,* and *dust* all refer to it, illustrating this awareness.

This poverty has prevented most black people from having many of the luxuries in life. Life is pretty much reduced to essentials. In such an environment, then, certain material items tend to have special significance and status. For example, *knits, sack, thick 'n thins,* and *Brooks* reflect a black awareness of clothes. *Clean, pressed,* and *tough fit,* all allude to having nice clothes or being well dressed.

Cars, especially large and expensive cars, also have high status value, and again, the vocabulary makes this apparent. *Hog, rodda,* and *L.D.* are all synonyms for a Cadillac, and a *Deuce and a Quarter* indicates a Buick Electra 225.

Though less expensive, soul records are of considerable worth to many younger black people. It was never difficult to get music for a party with the students at school, for many of them, despite their limited means, had what amounted to libraries of *jams, wax, sounds,* or *sides.*

It is quite obvious that stylishness and desirability in appearance are accorded much status in the culture. But it goes beyond material things. Attractiveness and character magnetism are also held in high esteem. A vast number of terms refer to stylishness in either a personal or a material sense. *Hip, cool, with it, way in, fine, sharp, dapt, mellow, mean, slick, tough, together, bad, right on, game,* and *out of sight* are all used to indicate something or someone appealing, in vogue, attractive.

On a less pleasant note, being victimized and preyed upon by the wider society is central to black American life. Deadly poverty, exploitation, unequal treatment, inadequate housing, poor police protection, crowded living conditions, and substandard city services have all taken a heavy toll on black people. Degradation, desperation, frustration, anger, fear, exhaustion, distrust, and worst of all, perhaps, hopelessness are all common to the black experience. Such a situation is physically and psychologically damaging, rendering people victims of such enemies as early death, violence, prostitution, drug addiction, and alcoholism. Indeed these destructive forces exist at all levels of society and in all areas of America, but they tend to afflict those with little political and financial power most severely. Many black people have heroically avoided these effects of deprivation, but not all have been successful. It is little wonder, then, that the first duty of many black families has been to survive amidst these deadly traps. In any case, the jargon reflects these sad conditions quite distinctly.

Black jargon contains a host of words referring to white people, many of them in an uncomplimentary way. Among these terms are *honky, Charlie, gray boy, cracker, Mickey Mouse, paddy,* and *monkey.* Closely associated with this attitude is an awareness of the ever present figures of authority in the schools, on the streets, and on the job. So acute is this awareness that the overall term *The Man* has emerged to refer to any person in authority. Police harassment and brutality is not unusual, and so terms like *The Man* and *pig* have come especially to mean a racist or unsympathetic law enforcement officer.

Black jargon indicates an intense awareness of reality and a tendency to deal with it in a no-nonsense fashion. *Tell it like it is* is one of the most frequently used phrases of all and clearly points to this preoccupation with directness and reality, while *right on* serves as an exclamation of sincere and unequivocal agreement or endorsement. Coupled with a consciousness of honesty and sincerity, is an acute awareness of insincerity and deceit. *Jive, jivetime, playing, running a game, whupping the game,* and *fronting* are among the many terms referring to attempts at insincerity and deception of one type or another.

Where exploitation, victimization, and discrimination exist, so does violence. The expressions *ripped off, burned,* and *blown away* all may refer to death by violence. The vocabulary also has plenty of terms to indicate weapons commonly used in violent acts. *Ax, blade, shiv,* and *edge* refer to knives, while *rod, piece,* and *heat* are synonyms for a gun. Fighting may be described as *ginning, thumping,* or *humbugging,* while being *lit up* or *fired on* means to be hit or struck by someone else.

§The black vocabulary having to do with marijuana and drugs is shared with the drug culture at large. *Joint, boo-reefer, grass, pot,* and *tea* all refer to marijuana, while the word *toys* refers to the equipment used by an addict. A *spike* is a hypodermic needle. To be a *user,* a *monkey,* or *on it,* is to be currently addicted, while *high, twisted,* and *nodding out* are a few of the terms alluding to the state of drug intoxication.

Prostitution and its effects have plagued black and white culture alike, and black jargon has many terms dealing with it. *Pimp* and *mack man* indicate a man who operates a ring of prostitution, while a *stable* is the fleet of prostitutes in his employ. That prostitutes and pimps are not highly regarded in many black areas is indicated by the fact that the word *pimp* is used to negatively describe anyone who attempts to use and abuse others. Wherever prostitution exists, so invariably does homosexuality, and such terms as *fag, butch, pure silk,* and *bulldagger* refer to various types.

Alcoholism is another universal problem, and among blacks, *oil, steam, juice, grapes, suds, grog, ignorant oil,* and *taste* are a few of the terms referring to it. To be drunk is to be *tight, wasted, high,* or *laid to the bone.* To *gusto* is to drink, and if one is a *budhead* he is a beer lover.

Above and beyond all else there exists a tremendous rallying point and positive trait of black culture—the bond of unity and sensitivity that is so much a part of blackness. Although individuality and personal differences are as great among black people as any other, to wear the visible badge of blackness in America is to be relegated to a peculiarly difficult plight—one that tends to have a cohesive effect. Black people have often wisely capitalized on this common status in a way that promotes unity. There are a number of terms, such as *soul brothers, soul sisters, boots,* and *members,* that unmistakably point to this sense of unity and common sensitivity. It has often been this spirit of fellowship which has been the difference between victory and defeat, success and failure, survival and destruction for many black people when facing the incredible barriers associated with being black in America.

When we see the many ways in which the vocabulary reflects the culture, the value of getting to know this jargon takes on additional importance. For learning black jargon can, as we have seen, bring great rewards in increased knowledge, wider cultural interest, and most of all, improved communication. And in a country in which better communication between the races is so desperately needed, one can enrich his life greatly by taking advantage of every opportunity to better communicate.

A Dictionary of Black Jargon

The following section is a dictionary of black jargon. Some of the words and phrases are exclusively black, others have long been in common use by many cultural groups. A large number were at one time used exclusively by black people but have since been appropriated by other groups and therefore come into wider usage. All of the terms, however, are used by various urban black groups in America, and are included for that reason.

Most of the terms are core or nationwide, but I have included some regionalisms from around the country as well. Regionalisms are very important, as they often "go national" after a short period of time.

To aid in clarity, the dictionary is cross-referenced and parts of speech are given for most of the terms. The problem of designating parts of speech for phrases was resolved by taking the entire phrase as a unit and assigning a part of speech on that basis.

Terms referring to drugs or sex have been kept to a minimum. Every culture has a host of such terms, and to attempt to include them would be an endless task of little or no value.

Obviously, no dictionary is complete. Terms are constantly being added as a vocabulary develops. The intention of this dictionary is to present the interested reader with an adequate example of black jargon with which to work.

A

Afro *n.* a bushy, kinky hairstyle popular in the black culture: *The cat's got a bad Afro.* See also *bush, fro.*

ain't nothin' to it a curt, resisting reply often given to "What's happening?" or "How are you?": *What's happenin', man? Ain't nothin' to it.* See also *you got it.*

Aunt Jane *n.* 1. a black female who is a traitor to her race. 2. a black woman who tries to live a white life style.

ax *n.* 1. a knife, usually serving as a weapon. See also *blade, edge.* 2. a saxophone or saxophone-like musical instrument.

B

baby *n.* 1. often used in conversation with another person to refer to him: *You got it, baby.* See also *man.* 2. friend; pal. See also *mellow.*

Babylon *n.* a pejorative term referring to the United States of America.

bad *adj.* 1. good; nice; desirable; appealing in character: *a bad fox.* See also *boss, cool.* 2. stylish; in vogue: *a bad weave.* See also *dapt, equipped.* 3. outstanding; brilliant: *a bad performance.* See also *out of sight, right on, the end.* 4. strong; brave; physically courageous: *a bad dude.*

bad mouth *v.* to slander, to verbally attempt to destroy another's reputation.

bad rags *n.* nice clothes; handsome or attractive attire: *The cat's got some bad rags.* See also *tough fit.*

bad scene *n.* 1. a negative or undesirable situation. See also *scene.* 2. a tragic occurrence: *It's a bad scene, man.*

barley *n.* beer: *He's got some barley.* See also *grog, hops, suds.*

bat *n.* a physically unattractive female. See also *bear, mullion.*

bear *n.* a physically repulsive man or woman. See also *mullion, snags.*

be's *v.* is; often is: *It be's that way sometimes.*

big daddy *n.* 1. a black person held in high esteem. 2. a friend with a powerful reputation.

black *n., adj.* —*n.* an Afro-American. See also *blood, brother, sister.* —*adj.* pertaining to Afro-American culture or society. See also *soul.*

black-eyed peas *n.* a type of bean vegetable which in cooked form is eaten by many black people. It is considered a soul food. See also *soul food.*

black power *n.* self-determination for black people in the political, economic, or social sphere.

black power handshake *n.* a popular gesture of greeting and unity among blacks, involving a handclasp by locking thumbs with one another. See also *power shake, soul shake.*

black power sign *n.* a clenched fist raised in the air. See also *black power, power to the people sign.*

blade *n.* 1. a knife or dagger often used as a weapon. See also *ax, edge.* 2. a razor. See also *shiv.*

blood *n.* 1. a fellow black person: *How many bloods go to school here?* See also *boots, brother, soul brother.* 2. a black person who is one's biological relative: *That's the blood, baby!* See also *seed.*

blowing z's *v.* to sleep; nap: *He's been blowing z's all day.* See also *cop z's, sack.*

blown away *v.* killed in a violent fashion, often by shooting. See also *burned, rip off.*

blow your mind *v.* 1. to psychologically overwhelm someone: *Didn't I blow your mind?* 2. to shock or greatly surprise a person: *I'll tell you something that'll blow your mind.* See also *psyche.*

blue-eyed soul brother *n.* a white male accepted by black people; a male Caucasian liked by black people.

blue-eyed soul sister *n.* a white woman assessed as agreeable to black people; a Caucasian female acceptable to black people.

boat *n.* a car; automobile. See also *wheels, ride, short.*

bogart *n., v.* —*n.* 1. a brawler; a bully. 2. a strong, physically aggressive person. —*v.* to throw an elbow in a fight.

bones *n.* dice. See also *galloping dominoes.*

boo-reefer *n.* marijuana. See also *herb, joint.*

boots *n.* 1. black people; Afro-Americans. See also *member, my*

58

people. 2. footwear; shoes: *some bad boots*. See also *kicks, stompers*.

boss *adj*. 1. fashionable; desirable; attractive: *some boss clothes*. See also *hip, right on*. 2. magnetic in character; socially adept: *a boss fox*. See also *game, tough*.

box *n*. 1. a phonograph; stereo. 2. a television set. See also *tube*. 3. a radio.

bread *n*. money—currency, coin, or check. See also *change, lettuce, scratch*.

bricking *v*. to throw bricks as in a civil disorder.

brim *n*. a hat; apparel to be worn on the head: *Let me take your brim, mellow*. See also *lid, sky piece*.

Brooks *n*. an expensive or attractive shirt, often made by the Brooks Brothers Company. See also *knits*.

brother *n*. 1. a fellow black male. See also *blood, member, soul brother*. 2. any male accepted by black people: *What's happening, brother?*

budhead *n*. a beer drinker; beer lover.

building *n*. a house; home; place of residence: *Gonna get me a building, man*. See also *crib, pad*.

bulldagger *n*. a female homosexual; lesbian. See also *butch, queen*.

burn *v*. 1. to steal; take something illegally. See also *cop, liberate*. 2. to drive an automobile fast. See also *sheen*. 3. to run fast. 4. to kill, often by shooting. See also *blown away, rip off*. 5. to shoot a gun. 6. to smoke marijuana. 7. to cook food. 8. to perform in an outstanding fashion. See also *do it to death, got down*. 9. to defeat someone. See also *burned out, shot down*.

burned out *v*. to lose; be defeated: *Man, they got burned out!* See also *burn, shot down*.

bush *n*. a large, kinky, bushy hairstyle. See also *fro, natural*.

busted *v*. 1. to be caught or arrested for performing a misdeed. See also *popped*. 2. to be raided by the police: *The joint was busted*.

busting suds *v*. to wash dishes.

butch *n*. a lesbian or a female homosexual. See also *queen, stud*.

buttwoopin' *n*. a spanking; a paddling: *I'll give you a buttwoopin'*. See also *whup, woop*.

C

cabbage *n.* money in any form. See also *dust, pounds, slack.*

capped *v.* outdid; did better, often referring to a verbal exchange: *He capped you.* See also *put down.*

cat *n.* a black or white male person; ordinary man or boy: *a slick cat.* See also *dude, nail.*

change *n.* money. See also *jack, line, scratch.*

Charlie *n.* 1. a white person; a Caucasian. See also *whitey, gray broad, gray dude.* 2. white society in general: *Charlie doesn't dig that.* See also *WASP.*

chilled *v.* to be satirized; ridiculed. See also *playing the dozens, squaring out.* 2. to be coldly rejected; ignored: *He really got chilled.* See also *iced, ig.*

chitlins *n.* a soul food consisting of the cooked large intestines of pigs. See also *chitterlings, soul food.*

chits *n.* a popular cooked food of pig intestines. See also *chitlins, soul food.*

chitterlings *n.* large intestines of pigs. It is included in the diet of many black people and considered a type of soul food. See also *chits, soul food.*

chops *n.* 1. teeth. 2. lips. See also *coffee coolers, jibs.*

chump (you) off *v.* to verbally defeat someone; to get the better of one in a battle of words: *Aw, that cat will chump you off.* See also *chilled, come down on.*

clean *adj.* well dressed, attractively attired: *The dude is clean, man.* See also *pressed, tacked down.*

coffee coolers *n.* the lips of a black person. See also *chops, crumb crushers.*

coke *n.* cocaine.

collard greens *n.* a green, leafy vegetable which in cooked form is common to the diet of many black people. It is considered a soul food. See also *greens, soul food.*

collegiate *n.* a black hairstyle in which the hair is cut short and close to the head.

come down on *v.* 1. to harass or oppose, often verbally: *He'll come down on you for that.* See also *get on your case, squaring out.* 2. to fight; physically combat. See also *gin, went down on.*

comin' up v. growing up; maturing: *When I was comin' up.*

con game n. 1. the process of trying to influence a person by using trickery or deception, often through conversation. See also *game, program.* 2. the process of attempting to obtain goods and services by trying to swindle an apparently gullible person. See also *murphy, rip off.*

contact high n. the intoxicated state caused by being in the presence of people smoking marijuana. See also *high.*

cookie n. 1. a black person deemed disloyal to his race. See also *handkerchief head, Tonto.* 2. a black person who tries to live exactly as white people do. See also *Tom, Uncle Tom.*

cool adj. 1. enchanting or attractive in method; socially effective: *a cool dude.* 2. nice; favorable; enjoyable; pleasant: *a cool jam.* See also *bad, boss, hip, together.*

cool and slick adj. stylish and desirable; appealing and socially attractive: *He's a cool and slick mellow.* See also *cool, slick.*

cool it v. 1. an imperative expression meaning to relax or calm down: *Cool it, man!* See also *hang loose.* 2. to be quiet or peaceful.

cop v. 1. to take something. 2. to steal or pilfer; to get something wrongfully. See also *liberate, rip off.*

cop a squat v. to take a seat; sit down. See also *cop, squat.*

cop out v., n. —v. to avoid an issue. —n. cop-out—the act of avoiding a conflict: *That's a cop-out, man.*

cop z's v. to sleep; nap. See also *sack, z'sing.*

cornbread n. hot bread made out of cornmeal—a popular soul food. See also *soul food.*

couple of cents n. two dollars; a few dollars. See also *penny, nickel.*

cracker n. 1. an overt white racist. 2. a poor, white Southern hillbilly.

cram n., v. —n. a basketball stuff shot or dunk shot. —v. to stuff or dunk a basketball through a hoop.

crash v. to go to bed and sleep: *Got to crash and get some z's.* See also *cop z's, z'sing.*

creeping v. 1. to date or associate with the opposite sex. See also *game.* 2. to be unfaithful to one's spouse, fiancé, or regular dating partner.

cheddar

★ **crib** *n.* a house; living quarters; place to live: *Got to get back to my crib.* See also *building, pad.*

cribbing *v.* living; existing.

crumb cruncher *n.* a child; an infant. See also *crumb snatcher, split.*

crumb crushers *n.* lips. See also *coffee coolers, jibs.*

crumb snatcher *n.* a small child: *Got to take care of my crumb snatcher.* See also *crumb cruncher, split.*

cut *n.* a musical record: *Play that mellow cut, man.* See also *jam, sound, sides.*

cut me some slack *v.* 1. give me some money. See also *slack.* 2. give me a break. See also *slack.*

cut out *v.* to leave; depart. See also *drift, go north, hat up.*

cut sides *v.* to record; make musical records. See also *sides, wax.*

cyclops *n.* a television set; TV: *The dude's got an old cyclops.* See also *box, screen, tube.*

D

dap *n.* a rather sophisticated or complicated hand greeting used by many black people.

dapt *adj.* attractive; highly appealing. See also *equipped, out of sight.*

dashiki *n.* shirt-like, African attire worn by many black people.

dealt on (you) *v.* to take advantage of by outsmarting or double-crossing: *He sure dealt on you, baby.* See also *square up.*

decked *adj.* dressed well; attractively clothed: *The dude is decked tonight.* See also *clean, pressed, tacked down.*

Deuce and a Quarter *n.* the Buick Electra 225 automobile: *The cat's got a bad Deuce and a Quarter.* See also *ride, wheels.*

dewbaby *n.* a dark-skinned, black male. See also *midnight.*

★ **dig** *v.* 1. to understand; comprehend: *I can dig it.* See also *pick up, wise.* 2. to appreciate; to enjoy. 3. to listen; pay attention: *Dig this, man!*

dike *n.* a lesbian; female homosexual. See also *bulldagger, queen, butch.*

dime *n.* ten dollars; a ten-dollar bill. See also *nickel, penny.*

do *n.* 1. a person's hair. See also *wig.* 2. a processed hairstyle. See also *mop, process.*

doberman *n.* a dishonest or double-crossing person; a traitor: *The cat's a doberman!*

doin' it *v.* performing very well; handling something competently: *The cat is really doin' it.*

do it to death *v.* to perform in a remarkable fashion; to do something brilliantly: *They can do it to death!* See also *get it together, got down.*

dome *n.* a person's head: *Got hit on the dome.*

do-rag *n.* a head scarf often worn over a processed hairdo. See also *do, handkerchief head, process.*

down *adj.* appealing; socially attractive: *He's real down.* See also *cool, game.*

down home *n.* the South: *We're goin' down home next week.*

do (your) thing *v.* to act out your life without pretense; pursue your interests fully.

drapes *n.* clothes; attire; apparel: *some tough drapes.* See also *threads, weave, vines.*

drift *v.* to leave; go away: *Got to drift out of this place.* See also *slide, space, split.*

duck *n.* wine. See also *grapes, pluck.*

dude *n.* an ordinary fellow; a regular man or boy: *He's an all right dude.* See also *cat, stud.*

dukes *n.* a person's fists.

dukin' *v.* fighting; engaging in physical combat: *The dudes are dukin'!* See also *gin, thump.*

dungeon *n.* a room, often in a basement, used for dancing and partying: *The cat's got a bad dungeon.*

dust *n.* money. See also *bread, lettuce, pounds.*

dusted *v.* 1. to be defeated in a foot race: *He really got dusted.* See also *burn, burned out.* 2. to be knocked down in a fight. See also *floored.*

E

edge *n.* a knife or dagger, often employed as a weapon: *packin' an edge.* See also *ax, shiv.*

equipped *adj.* 1. stylish; fashionable: *The dude's equipped.* See also *bad, mellow.* 2. pleasurable; agreeable; desirable. See also *solid, toast.* 3. able; capable.

F

fabric *n.* clothes; wearing apparel; attire: *some boss fabric.* See also *rags, threads.*

fag *n.* 1. an effeminate male. See also *freak.* 2. a homosexual. See also *punk, pure silk.* 3. a cowardly person; a sissy: *He's a real fag, baby.*

fatherland *n.* 1. the local black community. See *homeland.* 2. Africa. See also *old country.*

fimpted *adj.* ugly, physically repulsive.

fine hammer *n.* a physically attractive female: *She's a fine hammer, mellow.* See also *fox, hammer, stallion.*

fired (me) up *v.* to strike another physically; to be hit as in a fight: *He fired me up!* See also *fired on, light up.*

fired on *v.* to hit or strike another physically: *The cat fired on him.* See also *light up, up side your head.*

fit *n.* 1. dress; clothes; apparel. See also *vines, weave.* 2. a suit; complete outfit. See also *front, vines.*

flick *n.* a movie; motion picture.

floorburners *n.* shoes; footwear. See also *kicks, stompers.*

floored *v.* knocked down physically; struck down as in a fight: *The dude floored him.* See also *dusted.*

fly *adj.* 1. neat in appearance; stylish-looking: *She's looking fly today.* See also *dapt, way in.* 2. attractive in manner; alluring in character: *She's really fly.* See also *down, with it.*

foot it *v.* to walk; journey on foot.

fox *n.* a very good-looking girl; beautiful female: *She's a bad little fox.* See also *fine hammer, momma.*

frames *n.* glasses: *I got some new frames.* See also *shades.*

freak *n.* 1. a homosexual. See also *punk, trick.* 2. a disturbingly effeminate male. See also *fag.* 3. a white hippie.

freeze *v.* 1. to stop moving; immobilize. 2. to be silent; be quiet. See also *cool it.*

fro *n.* a large, bushy hairstyle popular among black people. See also *Afro, natural.*

front *n.* a suit of clothes; an outfit: *a new front.* See also *fit, vines.*

fronting *v.* to exhibit false behavior; create a facade; to fake: *He's just fronting, man.* See also *woofing.*

funny *adj.* homosexual-like; having homosexual tendencies: *The cat is funny.*

fur *n.* a female wig; a hairpiece for women: *She's wearing the fur.* See also *rug.*

fuss *v.* to argue; verbally dispute. See also *get on your case.*

fuzz *n.* 1. hair on the head or face, usually a goatee: *The dude's got some fuzz.* 2. the police; a policeman. See also *pig, The Man.*

fuzzy *adj.* dull witted; mentally weak; stupid: *The cat's really fuzzy.* See also *lame, tired, unhip.*

G

galloping dominoes *n.* dice. See also *bones.*

game *n., v., adj.* —*n.* 1. a manipulative attempt: *to run a game.* See also *con game, program.* 2. the process of attracting a member of the opposite sex; the courting process. —*v.* to attract a member of the opposite sex: *to game after her.* See also *rap.* —*adj.* charming; socially adept: *a game dude.* See also *together, with it.*

gangbangers *n.* hoodlums; violent gang members: *The gangbangers got that cat.*

gangbanging *v.* fighting, especially as a group. See also *gin, humbugging.*

★ **gangsters** *n.* cigarettes. See also *squares.*

gas *n.* 1. an unusual or rare person or thing: *He's a gas, man!* See also *way out.* 2. an amazing or surprising event: *It's a gas!* See also *too much.* 3. a very desirable or highly appealing thing. See also *cool, hip.* 4. a processed or straightened hairstyle. See also *do, mop, process.*

gashead *n.* 1. one who has a processed or straightened hairstyle. 2. a black person who is a traitor to the pride of his race: *He's a real gashead.* See also *handkerchief head, Tom, Tonto.*

get it on *v.* an imperative expression meaning to start; commence; begin the activity: *Get it on, man.*

get it together *v.* 1. to organize or prepare something: *We've got to get it together.* See also *together.* 2. to perform well: *They really can get it together.* See also *burn, do it to death.*

get on (your) case *v.* 1. to verbally harass or attack someone. See also *come down on, fuss.* 2. to verbally chastise or punish someone: *If you don't do it, he'll really get on your case.*

get over *v.* to succeed; get by: *I can get over without studying too much.*

gettin' on *v.* 1. reaching inebriation due to excessive drinking. 2. becoming dazed and intoxicated by using drugs. See also *gettin' off.*

gettin' off *v.* 1. becoming intoxicated through the use of drugs. 2. getting drunk by consuming alcohol. See *gettin' on.*

get yourself together *interj.* 1. to regain control of yourself; return to proper functioning. See also *together.* 2. to straighten out; reform your ways: *Man, you got to get yourself together.*

gig *n.* 1. a job; employment: *a hard gig.* See also *hame, thing.* 2. a party; joyous event. See also *set, thing.* 3. a dance: *a mellow gig.* See also *jump, set.*

gigging *v.* 1. working; laboring. See also *hustling.* 2. dancing. See also *jam, shucking and jiving.*

gin *v.* to fight; scuffle. See *come down on, thump.*

give me the jive *v.* hand over the stuff; deliver the material. See also *jive.*

going through changes *v.* 1. experiencing many alterations in outlook and life style; being inconsistent and unreliable: *She's really been going through changes.* See also *shaky, sometimesy.* 2. working hard; laboring: *I've been going through changes all day long.* See also *gigging, hustling.*

go north *interj.* to leave or depart, often used as a command: *Go north, man!* See also *drift, slide, split.*

gopher *n.* one who likes, desires, or appreciates something: *I've been a gopher forever after that.*

got down *v.* performed in a spectacular or outstanding way: *Man, they really got down and did it.* See also *burn, get it together.*

got it down *v.* 1. can do it well. 2. know it well. See also *dig.*

got (your) nose *v.* 1. to be in love. See also *strung out.* 2. to have someone else under your control through infatuation: *Sounds like she's really got your nose.* See also *nose open.*

grapes *n.* wine. See also *ignorant oil, smash.*

grass *n.* marijuana. See also *joint, stick.*

gray *adj.* white; Caucasian: *The cat is gray.*

gray broad *n.* a Caucasian female; white girl. See also *ofay, peckerwood, WASP.*

gray dude *n.* a Caucasian male; white man. See also *Mickey Mouse, monkey, paddy.*

grease *v.* to eat; dine: *Got to get back to the crib and grease.* See also *peck, scarf.*

greaser *n.* one who is eating food. See also *grease.*

greens *n.* green, leafy tops of vegetables grown underground, the cooked form of which is common to the diet of many black people and considered a soul food. See also *collard greens, mustard greens, soul food, turnip greens.*

greyhounding *v.* dating or socially pursuing a white person; associating across the sexes with a Caucasian: *The cat's always greyhounding.*

grip *v.* 1. to back down or yield, especially after boasting of one's courage: *Don't grip now, man.* 2. to beg; plead; place oneself at the mercy of another.

grits 'n grease *n.* hominy grits and bacon fat. Hominy grits is a grain food which when seasoned with bacon fat becomes a popular soul food. See also *soul food.*

grog *n.* beer. See also *gusto, suds.*

grub *n.* food.

grunt *n.* a meal; dinner. See also *grease.*

gusto *n., v.* —*n.* beer. See also *steam, suds.* —*v.* to drink beer: *Gonna go out and gusto tonight.*

guts *n.* large intestines of pigs, often prepared as a soul food. See also *chitlins, chitterlings, soul food.*

H

hame *n.* a job; vocation. See also *gig, thing.*

ham hocks *n.* parts of the hind legs of pigs which when cooked in combination with various vegetables become a popular soul food to many black people. See also *soul food.*

hammer *n.* 1. a female; girl. See also *leg, sister.* 2. one's girl friend; female companion. See also *mink, old lady.*

handkerchief head *n.* 1. a black male who has a processed hairstyle with a head scarf covering it. See also *process.* 2. a black male who is a traitor to his race. See also *cookie, Tom.*

hang loose *interj.* remain relaxed, unruffled, calm: *Hang loose, mellow.* See also *cool it, take it light.*

hardlegs *n.* a male child; a youth. See also *splib.*

hat up *v.* to go away; depart: *Got to hat up soon.* See also *cut out, drift, space.*

hawk *n.* the wind: *The hawk is strong tonight.*

heat *n.* a gun, usually functioning as a weapon: *The cat's got some heat.* See also *rod.*

heavy *adj.* 1. nice; favorable; enjoyable; pleasant: *a heavy time.* See also *bad, hip, together.* 2. stylish; attractive in appearance: *a heavy weave.* See also *boss, mellow, tough.*

herb *n.* marijuana. See also *boo-reefer, tea.*

high *adj.* 1. intoxicated through the use of drugs, especially marijuana. See also *in a nod, twisted.* 2. mild intoxication due to the use of alcohol, making one feel happy or less inhibited. See also *tight, wasted.*

highland *n.* the north side of the city, often where the black community is. See also *lowland.*

high yellow *n.* a light-skinned black person. See also *redbone, spotlight.*

hip *adj.* 1. to be knowledgeable; to understand; to be able to relate: *Are you hip to that?* See also *pick up, wise.* 2. stylish; fashionable. See also *boss, right on.* 3. attractive in manner; socially able: *The dude is hip.* See also *mean, slick.* 4. nice; enjoyable; favorable: *a hip joint.* See also *mellow, solid.*

hit *n., v. —n.* a puff of a cigarette; a drag from a cigarette: *taking a hit. —v.* to inhale while smoking a cigarette; puff on a cigarette.

hit the street *v.* to leave one's house or place of residence for the evening, often to go out on the town. See also *cut out, slide, split.*

hog *n.* 1. a Cadillac. See also *L.D., rodda.* 2. a motorcycle: *a big, loud hog.*

homeland *n.* 1. the black section of the city. See *fatherland, old country.* 2. Africa. See also *fatherland, old country.*

honky *n.* a white person; Caucasian. See also *Charlie, paddy, whitey.*

hood *n.* one's neighborhood: *Did it happen in the hood?*

68

hops n. beer: *He'll buy the hops.* See also *barley, grog, suds.*

hot dog n. a quick-tempered, unpopular person. See also *pig, trick.*

humbuggin' v. fighting; brawling: *The cats got to humbuggin', man.* See also *gangbanging, up side your head.*

hung up v. 1. to be stymied; unable to progress: *He's got himself hung up on that one.* 2. to be burdened with problems: *The fox is really hung up!*

hustling v. 1. working; laboring. See also *gigging.* 2. being aggressive and enterprising, often in an effort to make money quickly and easily. 3. prostituting. See also *turning tricks.*

I

I can handle it very common statement asserting one's ability or competence with regard to a given task or even challenge: *I can handle it, mellow.*

Iceberg Slim n. 1. a pimp; a person who deals in prostitution. See also *pimp, mack man.* 2. an unpopular person who tries to take advantage of or exploit others. See also *pimp.*

iced v. 1. to be refused by someone; to be rejected: *She really iced me, man!* See also *chilled, shot down.* 2. to be isolated by virtue of being ignored. See also *ig.*

ig v. to ignore; disregard: *trying to ig me.* See also *iced, shot down.*

ignorant oil n. 1. wine. See also *duck, joy juice.* 2. whiskey. See also *juice, oil.*

I mean I wish to say.

in a nod adj. intoxicated through the use of drugs: *The dude's in a nod.* See also *nodding out, twisted.*

international nigger n. a black person dressed in a variety of expensive, imported clothes, often perceived as trying to identify with everyone internationally while, in fact, failing to identify with anyone.

J

Jack n. 1. a male person. See also *Jim.* 2. money. See also *line, scratch, slack.*

jack up v. 1. to rob or hold up someone. 2. to beat someone up: *I'll jack up the dude.* See also *floored, up side your head, whup.*

jam *n., v.* —*n.* 1. a musical record: *a bad jam.* See also *sides, sound.* 2. a popular song. See also *sound.* —*v.* 1. to play an instrument intensely. See also *wail.* 2. to dance: *Gonna jam a little.* See also *jam back, gigging.*

jam back *v.* to dance: *Time to jam back, mellow.* See also *jam, shucking and jiving.*

jam session *n.* an informal get-together of jazz musicians at which they play for enjoyment.

jibs *n.* 1. lips: *It hit him in the jibs.* See also *coffee coolers, crumb crushers.* 2. buttocks.

Jim *n.* a male person. See also *Jack.*

jive *n., v., adj.* —*n.* 1. informal language; popular jargon; slang. 2. insincere talk: *Don't give me that jive.* 3. meaningless or foolish talk. —*v.* 1. to lie or deceive someone: *Don't try to jive me, man.* 2. tease; play. See also *playing.* —*adj.* stupid; out of style. See also *lame, uncool, unhip.*

jivetime *adj.* 1. insincere; not serious: *This is a jivetime place.* See also *jive.* 2. dishonest; deceptive: *a jivetime dude.* 3. ignorant; dull-witted. See also *fuzzy, lame, tired.*

Johns *n.* a prostitute's customers.

joint *n.* 1. marijuana. See also *pot, tea.* 2. a bar; tavern. 3. a hangout.

joy juice *n.* 1. wine. See also *grapes, juice.* 2. whiskey. See also *ignorant oil, juice.*

juice *n.* 1. wine. See also *duck, smash.* 2. whiskey. See also *joy juice, steam.*

jump *n.* 1. a dance. See also *gig, set.* 2. a fight. See also *rumble, swing out.*

jumpers *n.* gym shoes; tennis shoes: *He's got new jumpers.*

K

keep the faith *interj.* be loyal; remain true.

kicks *n.* shoes; footwear: *Got some new kicks today.* See also *floorburners, stompers.*

King's English *n.* standard English; formal American language: *I got to use the King's English, baby.*

knits *n.* 1. shirts. See also *Brooks.* 2. sweaters.

L

L7 *adj., n.* —*adj.* completely out of style; not like the group. See also *uncool, way out.* —*n.* a square; unpopular person; one who is not like the group: *a real L7.* See also *square, trick.*

L.D. *n.* a Cadillac Eldorado. See also *hog, rodda.*

Lady Day *n.* Billie Holliday: *I got a Lady Day jam.*

laid crib *n.* a nice house; attractive residence. See also *crib, pad.*

laid to the bone *adj.* drunk; inebriated: *The dude was laid to the bone.* See also *tight, wasted.*

laid up *adj.* sick; unable to engage in one's regular activities due to illness.

lame *adj.* 1. uninteresting; dull; boring: *a lame gig.* See also *off the wall, tired.* 2. ignorant; stupid. See also *fuzzy, unhip.* 3. not like the others; not fashionable; out of style: *a lame dude.* See also *L7, square.*

later *interj.* farewell; goodby. See also *play it cool, take it light.*

lay it on *v.* to explain clearly and fully; to relate something candidly and completely: *Lay it on me, man.* See also *tell it like it is, whip it on.*

lay up *v.* to relax; take it easy. See also *hang loose, take it light.*

leg *n.* a girl; female. See also *hammer, soul sister.*

lettuce *n.* money. See also *bread, change, cabbage.*

liberate *v.* to steal; take illegally or wrongfully. See also *burn, cop, rip off.*

lid *n.* a hat; wearing apparel for the head. See also *brim, sky piece.*

light up *v.* to hit someone, strike: *I'll light up the cat.* See also *fired on, up side your head.*

like man used as form of punctuation or as an exclamation: *Like man, it's out of sight.* See also *man.*

line *n.* money. See also *jack, pounds, slack.*

lip off *v.* to engage in backtalk; to verbally rebel.

lowland *n.* the south side of the city, often where the black area of the city is located. See also *highland.*

M

machine *n.* a car; automobile. See also *boat, wheels, short.*

macking v. to engage in conversation used by pimps to solicit women to work for them. See also *pimp talk.*

mack man n. a pimp; one who operates in prostitution. See also *Iceberg Slim, pimp.*

make it v. 1. to go away; leave. See also *cut out, drift, slide.* 2. to be successful in a romantic relationship: *We can make it, mellow.*

man n. 1. used as a greeting: *Hey man, what's happening?* 2. a friend; pal: *I can dig it, man.* See also *baby, mellow, pops.*

mannish adj. a black child's way of acting which is deemed rebellious and disrespectful by his mother: *Stop acting mannish!*

mean adj. 1. fashionable; attractive; in vogue: *a mean hog, man.* See also *right on, way in.* 2. socially effective; magnetic in manner: *a mean fox.* See also *down, game.*

mellow n., adj. —n. 1. a friend; pal: *What's happening, mellow?* See also *baby, man.* 2. an intimate acquaintance; close friend. 3. a loved one of the opposite sex: *She's my mellow.* See also *mink, old lady.* —adj. 1. intimate; close: *We're mellow.* See also *tight, uptight.* 2. attractive; stylish: *a mellow nail.* See also *game, tough.* 3. sweet; agreeable; nice: *having a mellow time.* See also *equipped, toast.*

member n. a black person; Afro-American. See also *black, brother, sister.*

mess v., n. —v. to bother; harass; interfere with either physically or verbally: *Don't mess with me.* See also *get on your case.* —n. mescaline: *The dude's into mess.*

Mickey Mouse adj., n. —adj. unimportant; irrelevant; uninteresting. See also *off the wall, tired.* —n. a Caucasian; white person. See also *honky, monkey, whitey.*

midnight n. a black person whose skin color is very dark. See also *dewbaby.*

mink n. a girl friend; female social companion. See also *hammer, old lady.*

momma n. a very attractive female; beautiful girl: *a real momma.* See also *fox, stallion.*

monkey n. 1. a Caucasian; white person: *They'll cover that monkey up.* See also *Mickey Mouse, peckerwood, WASP.* 2. a drug addict who is unable to break the habit: *The monkey got busted.* See also *user.* 3. a member of another group.

mop *n.* the processed hair of a black person. See also *pixie, process.*

mother-wit *n.* common sense; conventional wisdom: *Use the mother-wit, baby.*

mullion *n.* a physically unattractive person. See also *bat, bear, trollop.*

murphy *n.* a game or manipulative attempt by a hustler on a white person in order to get his money. See also *con game, rip off.*

mustard greens *n.* the green, leafy tops of the mustard plant which in cooked form are eaten by many black people as a soul food. See also *greens, soul food.*

my people *n.* 1. a gang or group to which one belongs. 2. black people; Afro-Americans. See also *boots, soul brother, soul sister.*

N

nail *n.* a male person; man: *a fine hammer and a mellow nail.* See also *cat, dude.*

natchie *n.* a poorly groomed black hairstyle; a sloppy natural.

natural *n.* 1. the normal, unstraightened hairstyle of a black person. 2. a large, bushy hairstyle. See also *Afro, bush.*

neck bones *n.* a soul food popular with many black people prepared from the neck bones of hogs. See also *soul food.*

Negro *n.* despite its normal biological and social connotation this term may also refer to one who is unfaithful to his race. See also *Tom, Uncle Tom.*

nickel *n.* five dollars; a five-dollar bill. See also *penny, scratch.*

nodding out *v.* to be in a drug stupor. See also *high, in a nod.*

nose open 1. to be in love. See also *strung out.* 2. to be greatly infatuated: *He's got his nose open.* See also *got your nose.*

nowhere *adj.* 1. not acceptable; unsatisfactory: *a nowhere joint.* See also *uncool, untogether.* 2. strange; unusual. See also *way out.*

O

O.G. *n.* Old Girl; mother: *My O.G. won't dig it.*

ofay *n.* a Caucasian; white person. See also *gray broad, gray dude, WASP.*

off *v.* 1. to maul; beat up someone: *I'll off that dude.* 2. to kill; take another's life. See also *rip off, burn.*

off the wall *adj.* irrelevant; unimportant; uninteresting: *an off the wall place.* See also *lame, Mickey Mouse, tired.*

oil *n.* 1. whiskey. See also *joy juice, steam.* 2. hard liquor in general. See also *taste.*

old country *n.* 1. the black area of a city. See also *fatherland, homeland.* 2. Africa. See also *fatherland, homeland.*

old lady *n.* 1. wife. 2. girl friend. See also *hammer, mink.*

on it *adj.* addicted to drugs. See also *strung out.*

oreo *n.* a black person who thinks from a white point of view; one who is, in effect, black on the outside and white on the inside. See also *cookie, Uncle Tom.*

out of sight *adj.* 1. spectacular; outstanding: *an out of sight flick.* See also *bad, right on, the end.* 2. extremely desirable; very stylish: *an out of sight fox.* See also *boss, mellow.*

P

P.R. *n.* a Puerto Rican. See also *parakeet.*

packin' *v.* 1. carrying a pistol: *The dude is packin', baby!* 2. carrying a knife.

pad *n.* a house or apartment; place of residence: *at his pad.* See also *building, crib.*

paddy *n.* a Caucasian; white person. See also *Charlie, honky, monkey.*

parakeet *n.* a Puerto Rican. See also *P.R.*

passport *n.* the permission of a gang to enter their territory. See also *turf.*

paying (your) dues *v.* enduring difficult experiences in order to be accepted as a genuine part of the group; undergoing the trials and tribulations necessary to being regarded by others as an authentic spokesman for, or member of a group: *It's all a part of paying your dues.*

peck *v.* 1. to eat; consume food: *Time to peck, man.* See also *grease, scarf*. 2. to playfully hug and kiss; neck. See also *slobbin'*.

peckerwood *n.* a Caucasian; white person. See also *gray dude, Mickey Mouse, whitey.*

peeped *v.* to read through a deceitful attempt; to perceive a fraudulent attempt in the making and hence avoid falling victim to it: *I peeped his game.*

peepers *n.* eyes.

penny *n.* a dollar; one-dollar bill. See also *couple of cents, nickel, dime.*

petrol *n.* automobile gasoline: *Need some bad petrol for the L.D.*

pick *n.* a comb used by black people for natural and Afro hairstyles.

pick up *v.* 1. to buy something; purchase. 2. to steal; take unlawfully. See also *cop, liberate.* 3. to understand; comprehend. See also *dig, wise.*

piece *n.* a gun, usually of the handgun variety. See also *heat, rod.*

pig *n.* 1. a racist policeman. See also *fuzz, The Man.* 2. a very unpopular person. See also *hot dog, trick.* 3. pork: *I had some bad pig tonight.*

pill *n.* a basketball: *He can really shoot the pill.*

pimp *n.* 1. a person who takes advantage of others to further his own ends. 2. one who profits by directing a ring of prostitution. See also *Iceberg Slim, mack man.*

pimp talk *n.* a conversation used by pimps to get women into their employ. See also *macking, pimp.*

pimp walk *n.* a type of slow strut associated with pimps. See also *pimp.*

pixie *n.* a processed or straightened hairstyle. See also *do, process.*

play *n.* 1. a greeting in which a person slaps another's palms. See also *slap five.* 2. a way of expressing approval through the palm-clapping action: *Give me a play on that.*

playing *v.* kidding; jesting; teasing: *I'm just playing.* See also *jive.*

playing the dozens *v.* verbally ridiculing or insulting one another, done by two or more persons often in a playful or jesting fashion; verbal one-upmanship involving two or more persons. See also *chilled, squaring out.*

play it cool *v., interj.* —*v.* to remain aware but controlled; to be relaxed and avoid foolish actions. It is often used as an expression of advice: *Remember, mellow, play it cool.* See also *hang loose.* —*interj.* an expression of parting; a farewell or goodby: *Play it cool, man.* See also *later, take it light.*

play the skin *v.* play the drums: *The dude can really play the skin.*

pluck *n.* wine. See also *duck, steam.*

popped *v.* to be arrested; apprehended: *They popped him last night.* See also *busted.*

pops *n.* an adult male person: *Take it light, pops.* See also *man.*

pot *n.* marijuana. See also *grass, tea.*

pounds *n.* money. See also *bread, change, slack.*

power shake *n.* a type of handshake, popular as a greeting and as a sign of unity and black power among black people. See also *black power.*

power to the people sign *n.* a fist held in the air. See also *black power, black power sign.*

prat *v.* to pretend to refuse; fake a rejection.

pressed *n.* neatly dressed; fashionably attired: *The cat is pressed, man!* See also *clean, tacked down.*

prez *n.* an acknowledged leader or power figure, often of a gang: *The prez doesn't dig it.*

process *n.* a hairstyle for a black male which results from straightening the normally bushy or kinky hair. See also *do, mop.*

processed mind *n.* a mentality which is alienated from black culture and tends to take on white attitudes: *He may have a natural, but he's still got a processed mind.* See also *cookie, oreo, process.*

program *n.* 1. life style; behavior pattern; method of operation: *That's his program.* See also *where you're coming from.* 2. a manipulative process; the process of deceitfully influencing: *I'm hip to his program, man.* See also *con game, game.*

psyche *v.* 1. to mentally outwit another; to outsmart someone. 2. to mentally intimidate; to mentally stymie: *I can psyche that dude.* See also *blow your mind.*

punk *n.* a homosexual. See also *fag, freak.*

pure silk *n.* a homosexual. See also *punk, trick.*

put down *n.* a verbal defeat; the experience of being verbally outdone or stymied: *a real put down.* See also *capped, chump you off.*

put it in layaway *v.* to save something; to preserve an object or experience for later.

Q

queen *n.* a beautiful female homosexual; attractive lesbian. See also *bulldagger, butch.*

R

raggedy *adj.* 1. poor; destitute; poverty-stricken: *His family is raggedy.* 2. shabby in appearance; tattered.

rags *n.* apparel; clothes; covering: *These are some bad rags.* See also *fabric, vines.*

raise *n., v.* —*n.* parents; guardians: *My raise isn't hip to it.* —*v.* to go; move: *Let's raise, man!*

rap *v., n.* —*v.* 1. to talk; converse: *We'll rap about that.* 2. to verbally flirt; verbally attempt to charm a member of the opposite sex: *He'll really rap to her.* See also *game.* —*n.* 1. a speech; address: *a bad rap.* 2. a conversation; dialogue: *We had a long rap.* 3. communication in general; interpersonal rapport: *a silent rap.*

redbone *n.* a black female with light skin color. See also *high yellow, spotlight.*

rep *n.* one's reputation, usually pertaining to a male and determined on the basis of physical toughness and aggressiveness: *The cat's got a bad rep.*

ride *n.* a car; automobile: *a tough ride.* See also *machine, sheen, tootmobile.*

right on *interj., adj.* —*interj.* 1. an expression of agreement or endorsement: *I say right on to that, mellow.* See also *solid.* 2. continue what you're saying: *Right on, brother.* —*adj.* 1. excellent; outstanding: *a right on job.* See also *out of sight, the end.* 2. fashionable; appealing: *a right on ride.* See also *fly, way in.*

rip off *v., n.* —*v.* 1. to steal; obtain wrongfully. See also *burn, cop.* 2. to kill violently. See also *blown away, burn.* 3. to destroy;

eliminate: *I'll rip off anything that gets in my way.* —*n.* an exploitive attempt; a swindle: *Man, that's a rip off.* See also *con game, murphy.*

rod *n.* a gun, often a handgun. See also *heat, piece.*

rodda *n.* a Cadillac. See also *hog, L.D.*

rough *adj.* attractive; fashionable; stylish; appealing: *a rough short.* See also *bad, boss, tough.*

rug *n.* a wig worn by females; a women's hairpiece: *an expensive rug.* See also *fur.*

rumble *n.* a gang fight; group conflict: *planning a rumble.* See also *jump, swing out.*

running a game *v.* attempting to cleverly manipulate; trying to influence someone through the use of trickery: *He's running a game on me.* See also *game, whupping the game.*

running (something) down *v.* explaining an issue; verbally relating a situation.

S

sack *n., v.* —*n.* 1. jacket; coat: *Where's my sack?* 2. bed. —*v.* to slumber, sleep. See also *blowing z's, z'sing.*

sapphire *n.* a derogatory name used to denote an unpopular black female: *She's a real sapphire, mellow.*

scarf *v.* to eat; devour food. See also *grease, peck.*

scene *n.* 1. place of an event; area of action: *Hit the scene.* 2. situation; predicament: *a wild scene.* See also *bad scene.*

scratch *n.* money. See also *cabbage, lettuce, pounds.*

scratching *v.* writing.

screen *n.* a television set; TV: *I've got a bad, new screen.* See also *box, cyclops, tube.*

seed *n.* 1. a baseball. 2. offspring; son or daughter. See also *blood.*

set *n.* 1. a party. See also *gig, thing.* 2. a dance. See also *gig, jump.*

seven-o *n.* Seventieth Street; *He lives on seven-o.* See also *six-tray.*

shack *n.* a home; apartment; place of residence: *I've got to split for my shack.* See also *building, crib, pad.*

shades *n.* glasses, usually sunglasses. See also *tints.*

shakin' *n.* happening; event; going on; an occurrence. See also *what's happening?*

shaky *adj.* 1. inconsistent in behavior; erratic: *She's shaky, man.* See also *going through changes, sometimesy.* 2. mentally mixed up: *His head is shaky.* See also *fuzzy, lame.*

sheen *n., v.* —*n.* a car; automobile. See also *boat, machine, wheels.* —*v.* to drive a car. See also *burn.*

she's there an expression indicating that a young woman understands and can really relate to a man. See also *hip.*

shiv *n.* 1. a knife; dagger. See also *ax, edge.* 2. a razor. See also *blade.* 3. a sharp instrument: *Man, that's a bad shiv.*

short *n.* a car; automobile: *a bad little short.* See also *ride, sheen, tootmobile.*

shot down *v.* 1. to be defeated; conquered. See also *burn, burned out.* 2. to be rejected; refused: *He was shot down by her last night.* See also *chilled, iced.*

shucking and jiving *v.* 1. being lazy; procrastinating: *He's always shucking and jiving.* 2. dancing. See also *gigging, jam back.*

side *n.* area or side of town usually where the black community is located: *going back to the side tonight.* See also *homeland, fatherland.*

sides *n.* records; record albums: *Got some mellow sides, baby.* See also *cut loose, jam, sounds.*

silks *n.* 1. nylon socks. See also *thick 'n thins.* 2. attractive acetate handkerchiefs.

sister *n.* a fellow black woman: *What's happening, sister?* See also *member, soul sister.*

six-tray *n.* Sixty-third Street: *on the corner of six-tray.* See also *seven-o.*

skimmer *n.* a hat; apparel for the head: *a mellow little skimmer.* See also *brim, lid, sky piece.*

skis *n.* very large shoes; large-size footwear. See also *kicks, stompers.*

sky piece *n.* a hat; headwear: *Here's your sky piece.* See also *brim, lid.*

slack *n.* 1. money. See also *bread, cabbage, line.* 2. a break; opportunity.

slap five *v.* to slap another's palms. This action has approximately the same significance as the wider society's handshake. See also *play*.

slick *adj.* charming or attractive in manner; socially adept: *a cool and slick dude.* See also *cool, down.*

slide *v.* to leave; depart: *Got to slide on out of here.* See also *cut out, drift, hat up.*

slobbin' *v.* lightly hugging and kissing; necking. See also *peck.*

smack *n.* heroin.

smash *n.* wine. See also *joy juice, juice.*

smoke *v.* to use marijuana: *Does he smoke?*

snags *n.* ugly, physically repulsive females; unrefined females. See also *bat, trollop.*

solid *adj., interj.* —*adj.* agreeable; good; desirable. See also *cool, mellow.* —*interj.* an exclamation of agreement or understanding: *Solid, mellow.* See also *right on.*

sometimesy *adj.* inconsistent in one's personality; moody: *She's sometimesy.* See also *going through changes, shaky.*

soul *n., adj.* —*n.* black or Afro-American culture. —*adj.* pertaining to black or Afro-American culture. See also *black.*

soul brother *n.* a black or Afro-American male: *Bring a soul brother.* See also *blood, brother, member.*

soul dancing *v.* dancing in styles which are peculiar and popular to black people and their culture.

soul food *n.* food peculiar and popular to black culture and the diets of many black people. See also *black-eyed peas, chitterlings, collard greens, cornbread, greens, grits 'n grease, mustard greens, neck bones, sweet potato pie, turnip greens, ham hocks.*

soul music *n.* uniquely black music composed by black musicians, which transmits much of the culture and feeling of blackness.

soul shake *n.* popular thumb-locking handclasp used to symbolize unity and greeting among black people. See also *black power handshake, power shake.*

soul sister *n.* a black female. See also *black, sister.*

sound *n.* 1. a musical record. See also *jam, wax.* 2. a popular song: *a bad sound.* See also *jam.*

space *v.* to leave; go away: *Got to space now.* See also *cut out, make it, split.*

spike *n.* 1. a needle, usually a hypodermic needle. 2. an eye dropper.

splash *v., n.* —*v.* to take a bath. —*n.* a bath.

splib *n.* a black child. See also *crumb cruncher, crumb snatcher.*

split *v.* to leave; depart: *Time to split.* See also *drift, hat up, slide.*

spotlight *n.* a light-skinned black female. See also *high yellow, redbone.*

square *adj., n.* —*adj.* 1. stupid; unable to understand: *a square cat.* See also *fuzzy, lame.* 2. not able to fit in; not like the other people. See also *tired, untogether.* —*n.* 1. an ignorant person. See also *L7.* 2. a person who is not socially acceptable: *He's a square.* See also *hot dog, trick.*

squares *n.* cigarettes. See also *gangsters.*

square up *v.* to doublecross; betray: *She'll square up on you.* See also *dealt on you.*

squaring out *v.* ridiculing or satirizing a person in his presence; verbally embarrassing another. See also *chilled, playing the dozens.*

squat *v., n.,* —*v.* to sit. —*n.* a seat; place to sit. See also *cop a squat.*

stable *n.* the group of females who work for a pimp.

stalks *n.* legs.

stallion *n.* a physically appealing female; beautiful girl. See also *fine hammer, fox.*

steady on the case *v.* to be persistently pursuing an issue; continue working at something: *He's steady on the case, man.*

steam *n.* 1. beer. See also *grog, gusto.* 2. wine. See also *duck, grapes.*

steerer *n.* one who directs or steers customers to another, often for an illegal enterprise.

step *v.* 1. to dance: *He can really step.* See also *gigging, jam back.* 2. to run: *The cat will really step out of here.*

stick *n.* a marijuana cigarette. See also *boo-reefer, joint.*

stompers *n.* shoes; footwear: *Got some new stompers.* See also *floorburners, kicks.*

straight *adj.* 1. permissible; acceptable: *The dude is straight.* 2. nice; friendly. 3. honest; genuine.

strung out *adj.* 1. in love; deeply infatuated: *He's strung out on* *her.* See also *got your nose, nose open.* 2. addicted to drugs. See also *on it.*

stud *n.* 1. a man; boy. See also *dude, nail.* 2. a homosexual female. See also *butch, queen.*

suds *n.* beer. See also *gusto, steam.*

sweet potato pie *n.* a soul food dessert popular among black people which is made largely of sweet potatoes or yams and which tastes very similar to pumpkin pie. See also *soul food.*

swing *v.* to have a good or merry time as at a party: *to swing a little.*

swing out *n.* a fight between gangs or gang members. See also *jump, rumble.*

T

T.C.B. *v.* take care of business; move into action: *Going to T.C.B. on that.*

tack *n.* a clever or smart man.

tacked down *adj.* attractively dressed; neatly attired: *The dude is tacked down.* See also *clean, pressed.*

take it light *interj.* an expression often used in parting. Means "take it easy": *Take it light, mellow.* See also *cool it, hang loose.*

taste *n.* 1. whiskey. See also *ignorant oil, juice.* 2. alcoholic beverages in general. See also *oil.*

tea *n.* marijuana. See also *grass, pot.*

teach *n.* a male or female who reminds one of an unpopular school teacher because of the authority such a person wields.

tell it like it is *v.* to explain in an honest, candid, and complete form with no reservations; to relate something fully and frankly without regard to the way it will be received: *Tell it like it is, baby!* See also *lay it on, whip it on.*

the end *adj.* excellent; fantastic: *It's the end, man.* See also *bad, out of sight, right on.*

The Man *n.* 1. a white person in authority. 2. a policeman; law officer. See also *fuzz, pig.* 3. an authority figure. 4. a boss; employer. 5. the Establishment; the power structure. See also *Charlie.*

thick 'n thins *n.* a type of nylon socks, commonly worn and considered stylish by many black men. See also *silks.*

thing *n.* 1. talent; skill: *Singing's his thing.* 2. a hobby; interest; pastime: *Just playing basketball is my thing.* 3. an occupation; vocation: *Teaching is his thing.* See also *gig, hame.* 4. a party; social get-together. See also *gig, set.*

thinks he's pretty a much used pejorative phrase denoting someone who has an inflated view of his own stylishness of appearance or manner: *That dude thinks he's pretty.*

threads *n.* clothes; apparel; dress: *Got some mellow threads.* See also *fit, rags.*

thump *v.* to fight; scuffle. See also *gin, up side your head.*

tight *adj.* 1. intimate; close: *We're tight.* See also *mellow, uptight.* 2. angry; very upset: *Don't get tight, man.* See also *uptight, wind in his jaws.* 3. drunk; inebriated. See also *high, twisted.*

tight cheeks *adj.* extremely angry; incensed: *The dude had tight cheeks when he left.* See also *tight, uptight.*

tight jaws *adj.* furious; very angry: *I'm getting some tight jaws now.* See also *tight cheeks, wind in his jaws.*

tints *n.* 1. prescription glasses with colored lenses. 2. sunglasses: *The dude's got some bad tints.* See also *shades.*

tired *adj.* 1. stupid; unable to comprehend: *The cat is tired.* See also *fuzzy, lame.* 2. monotonous; boring. See also *Mickey Mouse, off the wall.* 3. not stylish; not acceptable to others. See also *uncool, untogether.*

toast *adj.* good; fine; acceptable. See also *cool, solid.*

together *adj.* 1. functioning very well; operating smoothly: *He's got himself together.* See also *get it together, get yourself together.* 2. stylish in manner; socially adept: *a together dude.* See also *bad, hip.* 3. fashionable; appealing: *a together outfit.* See also *boss, mean.* 4. pleasurable; favorable: *a together set.* See also *mellow, solid.*

Tom *n.* 1. a black male who is a disgrace to fellow black people: *He ain't no Tom!* See also *cookie, Tonto.* 2. a black man who tries to live a white life style. See also *handkerchief head, Uncle Tom.*

Tom and try *v.* to attempt to achieve a goal by being a traitor to one's race; to betray one's race in an effort to obtain a personal end: *I'm not going to Tom and try in order to make it.* See also *Tom.*

Tonto *n.* a black male who is untrue to his race. See also *handkerchief head, Uncle Tom.*

too much *adj.* overwhelming; unbelievable. See also *gas, way out.*

tootmobile *n.* a car; automobile. See also *boat, short, wheels.*

torch *n.* a large cigarette lighter.

tore up *adj.* 1. in tattered and bruised condition as after a fight: *Man, you're tore up.* 2. emotionally upset and angry. See also *tight, uptight.*

to the max *adv.* to the greatest extent; to the ultimate degree: *We did it to the max, baby.*

tough *adj.* 1. very desirable; extremely enjoyable: *a tough jam.* See also *equipped, together.* 2. attractive; physically desirable: *a tough short.* See also *fly, way in.* 3. stylish in manner; socially adept: *a tough dude.* See also *mean, with it.*

tough fit *n.* attractive clothes; nice-looking apparel: *Got a tough fit there, mellow.* See also *bad rags.*

toys *n.* a set of equipment used by drug addicts.

trick *n.* 1. an unpopular person. See also *hot dog, pig.* 2. a dishonest person. 3. a sexual deviant. 4. a prostitute. 5. a homosexual. See also *freak, pure silk.*

trollop *n.* an unpopular or physically unattractive female. See also *bear, snags.*

tube *n.* a television set. See also *box.*

turf *n.* a gang's territory.

turning tricks *v.* performing acts of prostitution. See also *hustling.*

turnip greens *n.* the green, leafy tops of turnips the cooked form of which is common as a soul food. See also *greens, soul food.*

twisted *adj.* 1. in a trance caused by drugs. See also *high, nodding out.* 2. intoxicated due to alcohol; inebriated. See also *laid to the bone, wasted.*

U

Uncle Tom *n.* 1. a black person who is disloyal to his own people. See also *cookie, Tom.* 2. a black person who attempts to take on a white style of living. See also *handkerchief head, Tom.*

uncool *adj.* 1. not appealing or magnetic in manner; not socially smooth: *He's so uncool!* See also *lame, unhip.* 2. not pleasurable; not pleasant or agreeable: *an uncool set.* See also *unhip, untogether.*

unhip *adj.* 1. not knowledgeable; not able to relate; not able to comprehend: *They're so unhip as to what's happening.* See also *lame, tired.* 2. not stylish or fashionable in manner: not socially adept: *The cat is really unhip.* See also *hip, square.* 3. not enjoyable or pleasant; not desirable: *an unhip place.* See also *uncool, untogether.*

untogether *adj.* 1. not functioning well; not operating smoothly: *He's untogether when it comes to that.* 2. not attractive in manner or socially skillful: *He's so untogether!* See also *square, tired.* 3. not in vogue; unappealing: *an untogether crib.* See also *lame.* 4. not pleasant or enjoyable: *The set was untogether.* See also *uncool, unhip.*

up side (your) head *v.* to physically strike or fight; scuffle: *I'm going to go up side your head.* See *come down on, fired on.*

uptight *adj.* 1. angry; furious: *He's really uptight, man.* See also *tight, tight jaws.* 2. rigid; tense; ill at ease. 3. very friendly; intimate. See also *mellow, tight.*

user *n.* one who is on drugs; a drug addict. See also *monkey.*

V

vacation *n.* a period spent in jail: *They gave the cat a vacation.*

vines *n.* 1. clothing; apparel: *some tough vines.* See also *fabric, weave, threads.* 2. a suit; an outfit. See also *fit, front.*

W

wail *v.* 1. to sing: *She can really wail, man.* 2. to play a musical instrument with great fervor. See also *jam.*

walk *v.* to drive toward the hoop in basketball: *Man, can that cat walk.*

war lord *n.* a gang member who sets the terms and arranges the details for a gang battle. See also *rumble, swing out.*

WASP *n.* a White Anglo-Saxon Protestant. See also *Charlie.* 2. any white person. See also *gray broad, gray dude, ofay.*

wasted *adj.* intoxicated; inebriated: *The dude was really wasted.* See also *laid to the bone, twisted.*

wax *n.* 1. chewing gum. 2. a musical record. See also *jam, sides.*

way in *adj.* very stylish; in vogue. See also *dapt, tough.*

way out *adj.* 1. not stylish; not fashionable. See also *lame, square.* 2. not comprehensible; not understandable. 3. very unusual; unbelievable; outlandish. See also *gas, nowhere.*

weak *adj.* 1. inadequate; inferior. 2. inappropriate; not timely.

weave *n.* clothes; attire; dress: *a mean weave.* See also *fabric, fit, threads.*

weeds *n.* plants; shrubs; garden foliage: *You got some bad weeds there, man.*

went down on *v.* fought with; scuffled with: *He went down on him.* See also *come down on, thump.*

what's going down? What's the situation? What's taking place? This phrase usually has negative connotations, referring to a situation in which people are being tricked, cheated or taken advantage of: *What's going down at school, man?* See also *bad scene.*

what's happening? *interj.* 1. a greeting synonymous with "hello": *What's happening, mellow?* 2. What's taking place? What's going on? See also *shakin', what's going down?*

wheels *n.* a car; automobile. See also *machine, sheen, short.*

where (you're) coming from 1. what you mean; what you're getting at; what you're saying. 2. one's point of view; the perspective out of which one is operating: *I don't know where you're coming from.* See also *program.*

whip it on *v.* to say something frankly and entirely; to explain something fully and without hesitation: *He'll whip it on you.* See also *lay it on, tell it like it is.*

whitey *n.* a Caucasian; white person. See also *Charlie, honky, paddy.*

whup *v.* 1. to spank; to physically strike in order to punish: *I'll whup your behind.* 2. to beat up as in a fight; to physically conquer: *I'll whup him.*

whupping the game *v.* 1. attempting to influence someone through the use of trickery, often verbal. See also *game, running a game.* 2. trying to gain materials and services from someone who appears as though he can be swindled. See also *con game, rip off.*

wig *n.* 1. a person's hair. See also *do.* 2. a crazy person; very unusual person: *a real wig.*

wind in his jaws *adj.* angry; extremely upset: *The cat's got wind in his jaws.* See also *tight cheeks, tight jaws.*

wise *v.* 1. to agree with; to approve. See also *with it.* 2. to understand; comprehend. See also *dig, pick up.*

with it *adj.* 1. on our side; in agreement with. See also *wise.* 2. stylish in manner; socially adept: *a with it dude.* See also *slick, together.*

woofing *v.* to threaten in the manner of a bluff: *You're just woofing, man.* See also *fronting.*

woop *v.* whup. See *whup.*

wow *interj.* a commonly used, sarcastic response ridiculing an excited statement made by another.

X

x-ray *v.* to look at closely; get a visible impression: *Gonna really x-ray the scene.*

Y

yea big an expression often coupled with a hand gesture to indicate a specific size: *It was yea big, baby.*

you ain't sayin' nothin' Your opinion is worthless; your words are of no substance or importance.

you better know it 1. a statement often emphasizing a given command with the implication that a form of enforcement exists. 2. a statement indicating that what precedes it is definitely true and accepted by all.

you got it a statement usually in response to the greeting "What's happening?" and often meaning that nothing is really happening that the other person does not understand: *What's happening, man? You got it.* See also *ain't nothin' to it.*

Z

z'sing *v.* sleeping; napping: *He's still z'sing.* See also *blowing z's, cop z's.*

Bibliography

Claerbaut, David. "Inner-City Jargon . . . ," unpublished master's thesis, University of Michigan, Ann Arbor, Michigan (1970).

Davis, Lucian. "Can You Dig It?" *California Teachers Association Journal,* LXV, No. 3 (1969), 19.

Deutsch, Martin, et al. *The Disadvantaged Child.* New York: Basic Books, Inc., 1967.

Goodman, Kenneth S. "Dialect Barriers to Reading Comprehension," *Teaching Black Children to Read,* ed. by Joan C. Baratz and Roger Schuy. Washington, D. C.: Center for Applied Linguistics, 1969, 14-28.

Green, William D. "Language and the Culturally Different," *English Journal,* LIV, No. 8 (1965), 724-740.

Grier, William H. and Price M. Cobbs. *Black Rage.* New York: Basic Books, Inc., 1968.

Herald, Clare and Lillian Barnes. "Hey Boy!" *Elementary English,* XLVI, No. 3 (1969), 263-265.

Herman, Sister M. "The 'Disadvantaged' Teacher," *The Catholic School Journal,* LXVII, No. 2 (1967), 25-26.

Kennedy, Wallace A., Vernon Van De Riet and James C. White, Jr. *The Standardization of the 1960 Revision of the Stanford-Binet Intelligence Scale on Negro Elementary School Children in the Southeastern United States.* Tallahassee, Florida: The Florida State University, 1961.

Labov, William. "Some Sources of Reading Problems," *Teaching Black Children to Read,* ed. by Joan C. Baratz and Roger W. Schuy. Washington, D. C.: Center for Applied Linguistics, 1969, 29-67.

Newton, Eunice Shaed. "Planning for the Language Development of Disadvantaged Children and Youth," *The Journal of Negro Education,* XXXIV, No. 2 (1965), 167-177.

Riessman, Frank. "The Culturally Deprived Child: A New View," *The Education Digest,* XXIX, No. 3 (1963), 12-15.

_____. "The Overlooked Positives of Disadvantaged Groups," *The Journal of Negro Education,* XXXIV, No. 2 (1965), 160-166.

Schuy, Roger W. "A Linguistic Background for Reading Materials," *Teaching Black Children to Read,* ed. by Joan C. Baratz and Roger W. Schuy. Washington, D. C.: Center for Applied Linguistics, 1969, 117-137.

Stewart, William A. "On the Use of Negro Dialect in the Teaching of Reading," *Teaching Black Children to Read,* ed. by Joan C. Baratz and Roger W. Schuy. Washington, D. C.: Center for Applied Linguistics, 1969, 156-219.

Trubowitz, Sidney. *A Handbook for Teaching in the Ghetto School.* Chicago: Quadrangle Books, 1968.

COMPLETED

INVENTORY 1983